I0816162

WHAT PEOPLE ARE SAYING ABOUT *BIBLE JOURNEY*

"*Bible Journey* is an excellent resource for anyone who wants to understand the biblical narrative and how it continues to have relevance today. This resource is an excellent companion and can serve as a quick overview of key themes in Scripture or a great introduction to studying the Bible a coherent narrative. It's a journey worth taking!"

—**Matt Lucas, D.A.**
President/CEO, Our Daily Bread Ministries

"In *Bible Journey*, Bryan Dolan illustrates the power of the Bible as the Word of God, and the architecture of the Bible as a historical document written through the millennium with a singularity of purpose... to teach the character of triune God. He writes with the wisdom of a teacher who remains a lifelong student. The reader who is new to the Bible and the one who has studied it at length will gain knowledge of the story and personal application to their story. We believe it to be one of the most important books we have read in the past decade."

—**Drs. R. Scott and Pamela Pyle**
Business and Social Entrepreneur and Physician
Author of *Anticipating Heaven,* respectively

BIBLE JOURNEY

Discovering *Your* Story in *God's* Story

Bryan Dolan

Carpenter's Son Publishing

Bible Journey: Discovering Your Story in God's Story
©2024 Bryan Dolan

All rights reserved. No part of this book may be reproduced or transmitted in any form or by any means, electronic or mechanical, including photocopying, recording, or by any information storage and retrieval system, without permission in writing from the copyright owner.

Published by Carpenter's Son Publishing, Franklin, Tennessee
Carpenterssonpublishing.com

Scripture taken from THE HOLY BIBLE, NEW INTERNATIONAL VERSION®, NIV® Copyright © 1973, 1978, 1984, 2011 by Biblica, Inc.™ Used by permission. All rights reserved worldwide

Interior Design by Suzanne Lawing

Printed in the United States of America

ISBN: 978-1-956370-45-4 (print)

FOREWORD

You have before you the words of someone with significant but hidden fingerprints on the world stage. Bryan Dolan stepped away from a key role in designing nuclear power plants to write what you're reading. Yes, quite a contrast on the surface, but both efforts involve stewarding and structuring powerful information.

As you begin to discover the book's richness and its progression and logical design, you will catch a glimpse of his structured genius—and the genius of the book's structure.

I have known Bryan for years and followed closely Bible Journey's development as an advisor. His partner is also brilliant—Dr. Tim Laniak. Though having a Harvard PhD in biblical studies doesn't guarantee one's worthwhile contribution, in this case there's an obvious correlation. From the selection of the section topics to the packed appendices, you'll find the best of both minds at work.

Like the fictional Max Montoya of *Princess Bride*, Bryan has given the long sunset of his life's best energies to this effort—including both his wealth and wisdom. Bryan also brings to mind a non-fictional character who also put kingdom causes over personal wealth, that is, the heralded non-missionary William Borden. Bryan and his wife Joyce, like Borden, have become rather single-minded about Bible Journey. Borden allegedly wrote three words in the back of his Bible at three different times before his early death in 1913, at age 25. "No Reserves. No Retreats. No Regrets."

Borden passed a year before World War I began. This book, and the expansive Bible Journey curriculum, comes to us at another important crossroads in history—a culture war that is attacking not only the foundations of our constitutional republic, but of the Christo-centric foundations of many institutions foundational for extended civility and meaningful discourse.

Bryan was proud to be a midshipman, trained at the prominent U.S. Naval Academy. I was fortunate to speak at its homecoming prayer breakfast, at his request, and saw its motto, *"Ex Scientia Tridens,"* Latin for "In Knowledge, Sea Power." With this book and its program, you'll find the manifestation of a related motto, that with biblical knowledge you'll see God's providence and power throughout history.

Jerry Pattengale, PhD
Author, Senior Advisor to the President,
Museum of the Bible,
and inaugural University Professor,
Indiana Wesleyan University

PREFACE

B*ible Journey: Discovering Your Story in God's Story* is an introductory book written for those who are inquisitive and wish to learn the Bible's story, as well as those who have been studying the Bible but have not discovered its larger story. It intentionally balances content with simplicity in order to retain one of the overall purposes of the book, which is to teach the overall story.

In my experience, many people do not realize there is a story taking place, some know this but decline to participate, and others want to participate but do not understand their role in the story. While none of us are the hero of the story—that role is reserved for Jesus—we are each uniquely gifted and equipped for a significant role in God's story. He has equipped each of us to be apostles, prophets, evangelists, shepherds, teachers or some other significant role.

While understanding the story is a key objective, it is my greater hope that you will grow your desire to go deeper into your study of God's Word as you complete your own individual story in the larger story.

ACKNOWLEDGEMENTS

This book draws heavily on the curriculum of Bible Journey (a multimedia, online, seminary-level Bible curriculum developed and guided by Dr. Timothy Laniak, a Bible scholar and former dean of Gordon-Conwell Theological Seminary, Charlotte). Since 2010, Dr. Laniak's work has guided thousands of Bible Journey explorers in a classroom setting and online. Dr. Laniak's expertise as a Bible scholar and a curriculum developer has made it possible for Bible Journey to meet a critical need for a free, worldwide training program for pastors, lay leaders and others.

This book would not be possible without the inspiration of the late Dr. Robert Cooley, an accomplished scholar, archeologist, researcher, professor, administrator and highly sought after educational consultant who gave generously of his time to teach the Bible at our church over a period of nine years. Dr. Cooley led numerous trips to the Holy Lands to provide us with an on-the-ground experiential learning opportunity, and he took a personal interest in mentoring me, Tim Laniak and many others. Bible Journey was born out of Dr. Cooley's vision for online learning.

I would like especially to thank Joyce, my faithful spouse, for her detailed editorial review and her prayerful support and encouragement.

CONTENTS

INTRODUCTION

Welcome to a journey through the Bible! In this journey, it is my hope that you discover your *own individual* story within the larger story of God and his people.

We are going to walk through a six-act play, a widely used format.[1, 2, 3, 4, 5, 6, 7] The vast majority of the content from the story is taken from Bible Journey (an online Bible learning program), and all graphics and images are owned by or licensed to Bible Journey.

---

1 Institute for Bible Reading, "A Sacred Saga: The Six-Act Drama of the Bible," accessed November 20, 2023, https://instituteforbiblereading.org/drama-of-the-bible/.

2 Vineyard Church Ann Arbor, "Introducing the Six-Act Story of the Bible," accessed November 20, 2023. https://annarborvineyard.org/resources/sermons/notes/the-drama-of-scripture-introduction/.

3 "The Bible as a Drama in 6 Acts," Quizlet, accessed November 20, 2023, https://quizlet.com/ca/224681000/the-bible-as-a-drama-in-6-acts-flash-cards/?setIdOrUsername=224681000.

4 "The Drama of the Bible in Six Acts," Biblica, accessed November 20, 2023, http://downloads.biblica.com/tbotb/docs/tbotb-drama-of-the-bible.pdf.

5 Awaken by Sam Radford, "The Bible: A Six-Act Play," accessed November 20, 2023, https://samradford.substack.com/p/the-bible-a-six-act-play-489ea02f88d9.

6 "How to Properly Read the Story of Scripture," Redeeming God, accessed November 20, 2023, https://redeeminggod.com/how-to-properly-read-the-story-of-scripture/.

7 Craig Bartholomew and Michael Goheen, *The Drama of Scripture* (Grand Rapids, MI: Baker Academic, 2004).

RESOURCES

There are two resources in the appendices to assist you through this journey. The first is an outline which includes some key takeaways from each act of the story. Since we will touch on quite a few aspects of the story, this outline should help you stay focused on the bigger picture. The second is a glossary of terms.

EXERCISE

Before proceeding, write down some high-level facts about the Bible. These can be statements about the Bible that you believe are true, or they can be simple facts such as the number of books, or the number of authors. Take some time to do this exercise. When you are finished, set the exercise aside and continue reading.

WORLDVIEWS

A worldview is how we see and interpret the world. We all have a worldview shaped by stories. If our worldview is not being shaped by God's story, the Bible, then what stories are shaping our worldview? Is it simply our family, friends, work, and other cultural influences? If the Bible is fragmented into little bits, then it will be absorbed into our cultural story. Our whole lives will be shaped by our cultural story rather than that of Scripture! We will be conformed to this world. By the time you finish reading this book, you will not only have a framework for understanding the biblical story, but you will also have a framework for dwelling in the story.

> ***"If we are not shaped by the Bible's story we will be shaped by another story, ... that considers apes to be our 'closest relatives' rather than seeing humankind as the crowning glory of God's creation: made in the image of God."***
>
> –Dr. Timothy Laniak[8]

---

8 Timothy S. Laniak, Bible Journey classroom notes, 2010.

THE STORY

The Bible tells one unfolding story of redemption: the redemption of all of creation. We are part of the ongoing story that has a past, present and future.

"I am profitably engaged in reading the Bible.
Take all of this Book that you can by reason and the
balance by faith, and you will live and die a better man.
It is the best Book which God has given to man."
–Abraham Lincoln[9]

Let's briefly lay out the story before we get into the details.

The Story

ACT 1 Creation: God Establishes His Kingdom
ACT 2 The Fall: Rebellion in the Kingdom
ACT 3 Redemption Initiated: God Chooses Israel
Interlude: Intertestamental Period
ACT 4 Redemption Accomplished: The Coming of the King
ACT 5 Mission of the Church: Spreading the News of the King
ACT 6 Redemption Completed: The Return of the King

© 2018 BibleJourney

Figure I.1, The Bibical Story

ACT 1 CREATION: GOD ESTABLISHES HIS KINGDOM

In Act 1, the creation story, God establishes his kingdom. The creation story introduces us to a transcendent God who spoke a good,

9 "Abraham Lincoln on Why You Need to Read the Bible," FaithPro.org, accessed October 5, 2023, https://faithpro.org/abraham-lincoln-on-why-you-need-to-read-the-bible/.

ordered world into existence and gave his image-bearers their unique role.

ACT 2 THE FALL: REBELLION IN THE KINGDOM

Act 2, the Fall, is a story of rebellion in the kingdom. The Fall tells us the story of two individuals who sought to become autonomous, and as a result radically altered the course of human history.

ACT 3 REDEMPTION INITIATED: GOD CHOOSES ISRAEL

In Act 3, the process of redemption is *initiated*, starting with the selection of Abraham, which leads to the nation of Israel. "The remainder of the Old Testament tells the story of how the Creator God called a people to be his partner in rescuing humanity and restoring all of creation."[10]

INTERLUDE: INTERTESTAMENTAL PERIOD

The Intertestamental Period is the time between the last book of the Old Testament, Malachi, and the Gospels. This is the period in which God was preparing the world for sending his Son.

ACT 4 REDEMPTION ACCOMPLISHED: THE COMING OF THE KING

In the Gospels, redemption is *accomplished* with the coming of the King. The long-awaited hero, Jesus Christ, fulfills God's promise to redeem the fallen world. Although Jesus brings the kingdom of God, it does not arrive all at once.

---

10 Dillon Thornton, *Long Story Short* (Eugene, OR: Wipf and Stock Publishers, 2022), 12.

ACT 5 MISSION OF THE CHURCH: SPREADING THE NEWS OF THE KING

Act 5 shows us the mission of the Church, which is to spread the good news of the King. Until he comes again, Jesus *commissions and empowers* his followers to witness about him to the entire world.

ACT 6 REDEMPTION COMPLETED: THE RETURN OF THE KING

The story ends with the *completion* of redemption when the King returns. We receive a new heaven and a new earth in which everything is restored, and we are once again face-to-face in the presence of the awesome Almighty.

The biblical narrative both reveals God's purpose *and* invites us to participate. So as we go through the story, you will see God's purpose for his people, but you will also want to understand and respond to his calling on *your* life.

DIVERSITY

With respect to purpose, the Bible tells one unfolding story of redemption—the redemption of all of creation. The story is progressive, rich, diverse, textured and includes a variety of literary genres.

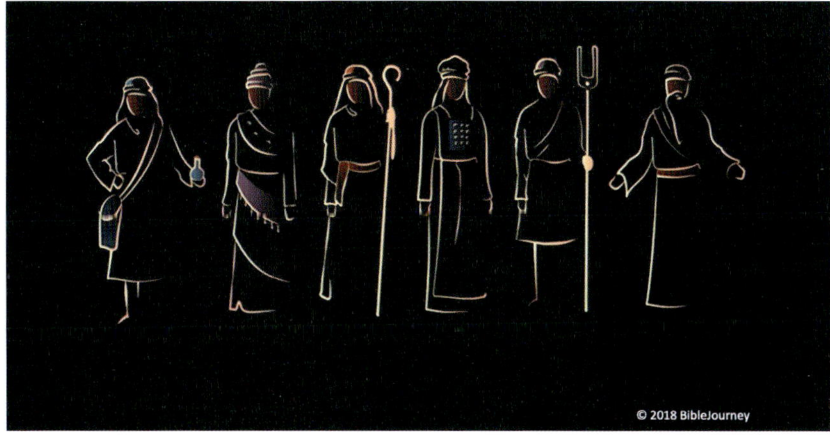

Figure I.2, Bibical Author Types

For example, the story includes biblical authors from many occupations over 1,500 years! As illustrated in Figure 1.2, its authors include physicians, kings, shepherds, priests, farmers, prophets, soldiers, fishermen, poets, scribes and musicians. It is begun by Moses in lonely Arabia, penned by kings in palaces, shepherds in tents and prisoners in prisons, and finished by John in isolation on the island of Patmos.[11]

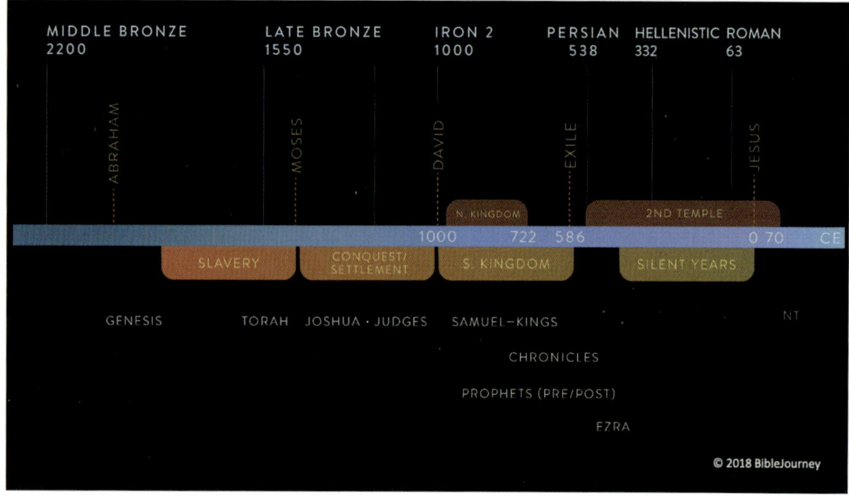

Figure I.3, Timeline of the Bible

TIMELINE

Before we get into the story itself, it might be helpful to highlight some key events and individuals in the Bible to give you a timeline on which to place the story. Notice that there are approximately 500-year intervals between Abraham, Moses, David, the Exile and Christ. There are also key 400-year intervals: Slavery, the Conquest and Settlement, the Northern and Southern Kingdoms and the 400 "Silent Years."

11 Timothy S. Laniak, Journey Prep video, accessed October 4, 2023, https://biblejourney.com.

If you remember these major dates, you will have a framework upon which you can more easily place other events. As an example, if you remember that David lived around 1000 BC, you will be able to recall that Solomon, his son, built the first Temple around 970 BC.

Some other key dates include:

- 722 BC: The fall of the Northern Kingdom, with the invasion of the Assyrians.
- 586 BC: The fall of the Southern Kingdom and the destruction of the first Temple.
- 539 BC: The Exile ended with the decree from the Persian King Cyrus.
- 516 BC: The second Temple was completed.

Thus, the Second Temple Period begins at the end of the Old Testament period and extends through the New Testament, ending with the destruction of the second Temple in AD 70.

COHESIVENESS

Although the Bible's timeline spans a period of 1,500 years and is written by over 40 authors with a variety of backgrounds, you will see that the story itself is one continuous story of God's relationship with his people over time. It is the story of God's pursuit of his people from the Garden of Eden to the Garden in Revelation, despite mankind's continual failure to be obedient to God's commands.

NESTED STORIES

Throughout the Bible, individual stories are bundled into larger stories which are integrated into cycles of stories and the larger biblical metanarrative, like onionskins.

Genesis, for example, is structured around the generations of key figures. Here are just a few examples: Adam (Genesis 5:1), Noah (6:9), Jacob (37:2). Within those generational main plots come subplots, like that of Lot in the larger Abraham story.

Figure I.4, Nested Stories

YOUR STORY

By the time we are finished, you will see how we are part of the ongoing story that has yet to reach its conclusion through time. Let's review the story in a little more detail.

"So great is my veneration for the Bible, that the earlier my children begin to read it the more confident will be my hopes that they will prove useful citizens to their country and respectable members of society."

–John Quincy Adams[12]

12 "John Quincy Adams Quotes," ChristianQuotes.info, accessed October 5, 2023, https://www.christianquotes.info/quotes-by-author/john-quincy-adams-quotes/.

Chapter 1

ACT 1 CREATION: GOD ESTABLISHES HIS KINGDOM

The story begins with the amazing opening scene of creation, in which God establishes his kingdom. The creation story introduces us to a transcendent God who spoke a good, ordered world into existence and gave his image-bearers their unique role. Genesis 1 shows us that God is eternal, one, distinct from creation, the sovereign King over creation, powerful, and personal.[13] God demonstrated his sovereign power by creating the ordered world from nothing (ex nihilo) and speaking the world into existence. The phrase "And God said" is repeated over and over.

> ***"It is mind-boggling to me that the Almighty power created everything I see; the Bible says that God created the entire universe just so he could create this galaxy just so he could create Earth so he could create human beings so he could create a family."***
>
> –Rick Warren[14]

13 Bartholomew and Goheen, *The Drama of Scripture*, 33–35.

14 "Rick Warren Quotes," Quote.org, accessed October 5, 2023, https://quote.org/quote/it-is-mindboggling-to-me-that-the-575975. Accessed October 5, 2023).

We know from John 1:1–3, "In the beginning was the Word, and the Word was with God, and the Word was God. He was with God in the beginning. Through him all things were made; without him nothing was made that has been made."

Humankind is a creature, has a relationship with God, and is made in his image (like God but not God), male and female (Genesis 1:26). So, we are *image-bearers,* which has significant implications in the way we view our fellow brothers and sisters.[15]

God's *intention* in creating the world was to dwell forever in the Garden with mankind, and we were to remain in relationship with him—with no pain, no suffering and no death.

From Genesis 1:28–30 and Genesis 2, we know that we were given the authority to *rule* over all of creation as God's responsible *stewards* on Earth, not exploiters, a loving rule with responsibility, accountability, development and care.

Finally, the world is good and ordered by God's Word. We see a refrain in Genesis that *everything* God made was good. "It was good." "It was good." "It was very good."

"What I see in the Bible ... is a recognition that all good things on Earth are God's, every good gift is from above. They are good if we recognize where they came from and if we treat them the way the Designer intended them to be treated."

–Philip Yancey[16]

THE CREATION STORY IN CONTEXT

There were other creation myths in the ancient Near East (ANE). For example, *The Enuma Elish (also known as The Seven Tablets of Creation)* is the Babylonian creation myth of the god Marduk's victory

15 Bartholomew and Goheen, 35–38.

16 "Phillip Yancey Quotes," AZ Quotes, accessed October 5, 2023, https://www.azquotes.com/quote/322319

over the forces of chaos and his establishment of order at the creation of the world.

However, there are some unique aspects of the biblical story that separate it from the other ANE stories. For example, the Genesis creation account is monotheistic, whereas ANE myths are all polytheistic. Genesis assumes the eternality and transcendence of God, whereas ANE myths talk about the origin of the gods. In Genesis, God was in complete control, and the original creation was very good (Genesis 1:31), whereas in ANE myths, the gods fight, and there is much evil in the process of creation. The God of Scripture is a nonsexual being, whereas the ANE gods are sexually active. Genesis 1–3 is history, as is all of Genesis, whereas ANE cosmologies devalued history.[17]

DOMAINS AND RULERS

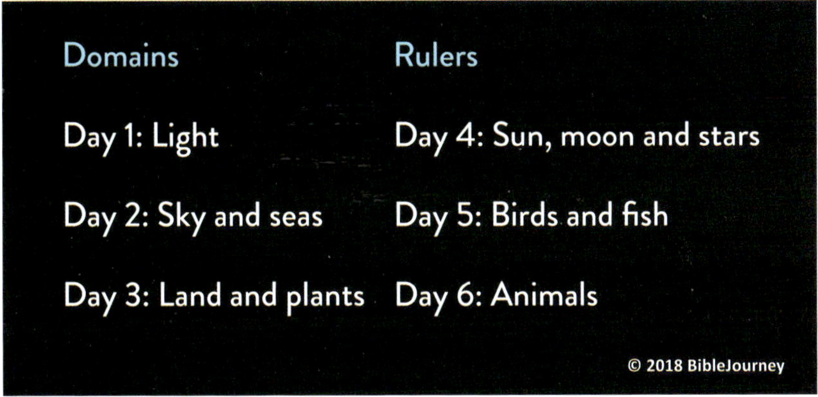

Figure 1.1, Domains and Rulers

Note that Genesis 1 is not only a sequential account of the seven days of creation, but that it also follows a movement from domains to rulers. For example, on day 1, God created light, and on day 4, he

17 John Oswalt, *The Bible Among the Myths* (Grand Rapids, MI: Zondervan, 2009), 21–185.

created the sun, moon and stars as rulers of that domain. On day 2, God created the sky and the seas, and on day 5, he created the birds and the fish. On day 3, God created the land and the plants, and on day 6, he created the animals and the humans as rulers.

GOD'S INTEREST AND FOCUS

Notice how the story starts with a wide-angle lens on the world (represented in brown). As we get further along in this discussion, we'll come back to this timeline to see how the lens changes focus but still keeps the entire world in mind.

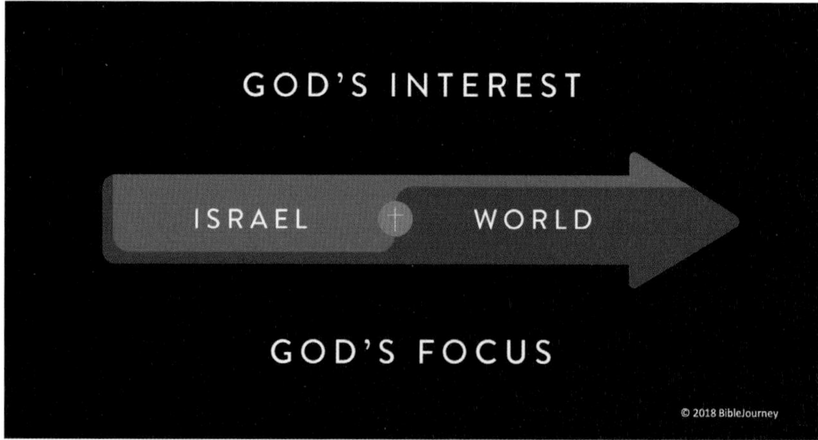

Figure 1.2, God's Interest and Focus

ACT 1 KEY TAKEAWAYS

- The creation story is about *how* the world was created, not *when* the world was created.
- Good science and good theology are compatible.
- Creation is characterized by beauty, order and purpose.
- God spoke the world into existence.
- God created man in his own image (sets humans apart), male and female.
- We are designed to reflect and showcase God's love.
- We are designed to reflect God's loving rule as we exercise dominion over his creation.
- It is our responsibility to be fruitful and multiply.
- The triune God is revealed: Father, Son and Holy Spirit.
- The creation story is unique amongst competing ancient Near Eastern (ANE) stories.

ACT 1 CHALLENGE QUESTION

Do you yourself reflect God's image, and do you treat all others as God's image-bearers?

ADDITIONAL REFLECTION QUESTIONS

- What did you find surprising about this part of the Bible story?
- What else did you find interesting about this part of the Bible story?
- How has this part of the Bible story challenged your thinking?
- How has this part of the Bible story shaped your worldview?
- What will you do differently as a result of what you learned?
- Who will you tell about what you have learned?

Chapter 2

ACT 2 THE FALL: REBELLION IN THE KINGDOM

Act 2, the Fall, tells us the story of two individuals who sought to become autonomous, and as a result "radically altered human nature and the course of human history."[18]

GOD'S INTENTION

As previously noted, God's intention in the creation story was to dwell with mankind forever. Mankind's only requirement was to not eat of the Tree of the Knowledge of Good and Evil.

CONSEQUENCES OF THE FALL

So what were the consequences? Mankind lost harmony with its maker, harmony with each other and harmony with creation. We were booted from the Garden, and God placed cherubim at the gate to prevent mankind from making its way back to the Tree of Life.

18 Thornton, 12.

THE NATURE OF SIN AND ITS CONSEQUENCES

Sin is essentially placing ourselves in charge. Sin is failure to acknowledge God as Lord of our lives and turning our backs on him. Put simply, sin is acting as though we have a better plan than God.

So, what are the results or consequences of sin? First, we alienate ourselves from God. In the case of Adam and Eve, they were banished from the Garden. Second, we have broken relations with each other, as evidenced by the finger-pointing between Adam and Eve. Third, death enters the picture. Here we see the words "... unto dust you shall return." Fourth, the ground becomes cursed in that mankind must painfully toil in order to earn food. Fifth, childbearing becomes painful, man will rule over his wife, and the soil will be full of bristles and thorns. So, we see very grave consequences from this original sin play themselves out throughout the remainder of the story.[19]

If you put yourself in God's position at this point in time, you might be thinking, *Okay, game over. Let's put the board and the game pieces back in the box, close the box, and take out another game.* And you would be perfectly justified in doing so.

A RELENTLESS GOD

So, is the story over? No!

While justly angry, God did not turn his back on a world bent on destruction.[20] God clothed Adam and Eve to cover their sinful condition. The animal skins required the shedding of blood, foreshadowing the future salvation act of Jesus Christ.

In fact, in Genesis 3:15 he even promised to crush the evil forces they unleashed.

---

19 Bartholomew and Goheen, 42-44.

20 "Our World Belongs to God," CRCNA (Grand Rapids, MI: CRC Publications, 1987), accessed October 5, 2023, https://missionworldview.com/wp-content/uploads/2020/06/ea8a85_f0ae5e48aa344ebfb43e88d5d37cb0b7.pdf.

After Adam and Eve were banished from the Garden, God kept his plan of redemption moving forward.

Don't miss the fact that we have a God who does not give up on us. Although Adam and Eve lost God's presence with them in the Garden and suffered these consequences, let's follow the storyline and see how God continues to pursue us despite our disobedience.

"RE-WORD" THEOLOGY

As you read through the story, you will see many of what we will call "re-words" that highlight God's persistence in his original design. God is the faithful one who recreates, rebuilds, renews, reforms, repairs, remembers, revives, and restores. While mankind fails at essentially every step of the story, God is the constantly faithful one who pursues his people and fully restores them when they turn back to him.

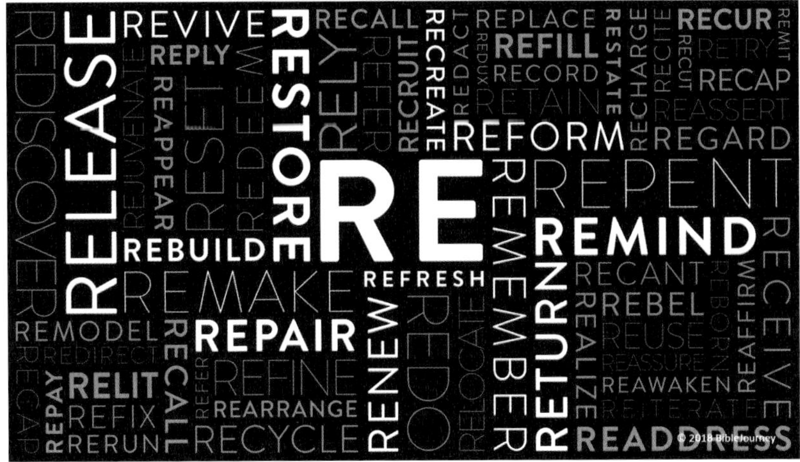

Figure 2.1, "Re-Word" Theology

ACT 2 KEY TAKEAWAYS

- Adam and Eve sought to become autonomous instead of depending upon their Creator for their understanding of the world and their place within it.
- The ordered world becomes chaotic.
- Consequences of the Fall:
    - o Alienation from God and the Garden (Genesis 3:8, 23)
    - o Damaged relations with each other (3:12, 16)
    - o Death (3:19)
    - o Non-human creation cursed (3:17)
    - o Creational task burdened (3:16–19)
- A sign of hope: The woman's offspring will one day defeat the serpent, although at great cost (Genesis 3:15).

ACT 2 CHALLENGE QUESTION

What are the gods which need to be removed from your life—money, power, drugs/alcohol, work, self-esteem?

ADDITIONAL REFLECTION QUESTIONS

- What did you find surprising about this part of the Bible story?
- What else did you find interesting about this part of the Bible story?
- How has this part of the Bible story challenged your thinking?
- How has this part of the Bible story shaped your worldview?
- What will you do differently as a result of what you learned?
- Who will you tell about what you have learned?

Chapter 3

ACT 3 REDEMPTION INITIATED: GOD CHOOSES ISRAEL

The story continues in Act 3 with God's initiation of redemption of his people through his choice of Abraham, which led to the nation of Israel.

Act 3 contains two scenes:

- Scene One: A People for the King
- Scene Two: A Land for His People

SCENE ONE: A PEOPLE FOR THE KING

Let's examine Scene One in two periods, which we will call the Universal Period and the Patriarchal Period.

UNIVERSAL PERIOD (GENESIS 3 11)

During the Universal Period, we see the origins of a number of things, including family and culture. However, this time period is polluted by sin.

So once again we see mankind's failure to act responsibly in relationship to God, and the consequences are severe. The Earth is flooded, and almost everything is destroyed, but once again God keeps his plan moving forward. In this case, God preserves a remnant through Noah, his family, and representatives of other aspects of creation.

Even after the Flood, we see mankind try to make a name (or *shem*) for itself at Babel. Once again, God's judgment comes swiftly in the form of confusion of language and scattering.

PATRIARCHAL PERIOD (GENESIS 12–50)

The book of Genesis has a hinge between Genesis 11 and 12. In Genesis 12, notice how the lens of the camera narrows from the entire world to the nation of Israel, while still keeping the entire world in view.

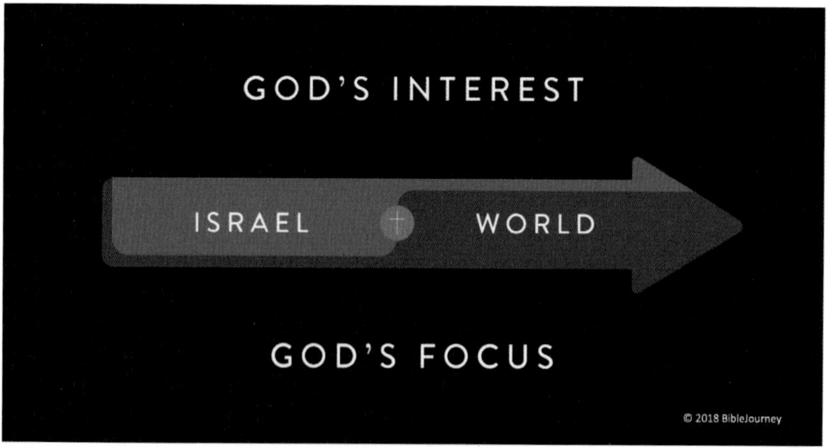

Figure 3.1, God's Interest and Focus

We are introduced to Abram, who was called from Ur, a city at the eastern end of the Fertile Crescent, the green band around the top of the Arabian Peninsula in Figure 3.2.

Abram was asked to leave everything behind, including his home, and follow God.

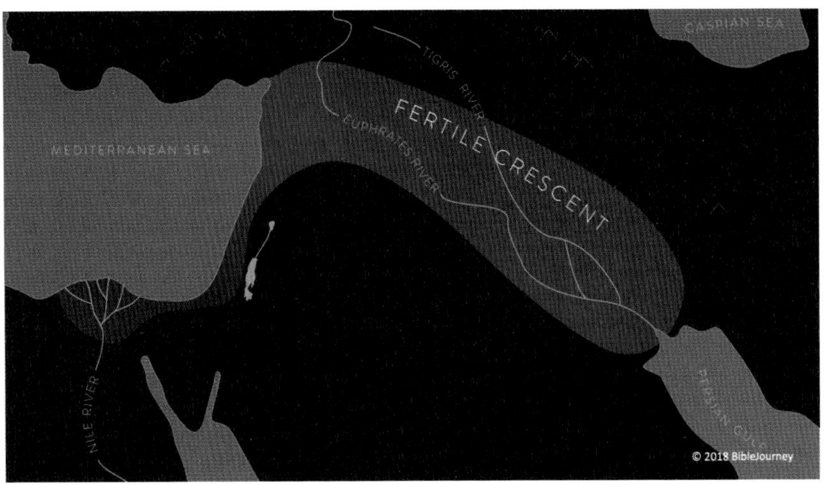

Figure 3.2, The Fertile Crescent

On his journey to the Promised Land, Abram traveled the Fertile Crescent.

In Genesis 12, we see an audacious promise from God to Abraham in which he will be a blessing to the world. The covenant will be established in Genesis 15 and confirmed in Genesis 17. In later chapters of Genesis, the covenant will be repeated to the other patriarchs, Isaac and Jacob. Jacob's name is changed to Israel, from which we get the nation of Israel.

As we follow the story, we'll see that God was not simply being generous to one person or one family. God's purpose in selecting Abraham, and Israel, was for them to be a light to the nations, so that everyone, both Jew and Gentile, would have a chance to become part of his family.

"The remainder of the Old Testament tells the story of how the Creator God called a people to be his partner in rescuing humanity and restoring all of creation."

–Dillon Thornton[21]

21 Thornton, 12.

EXODUS: THE FORMATION OF GOD'S PEOPLE

The story continues in the book of Exodus. God forms his people in a two-step process. In step one, God reaches down into Egypt and rescues his people. Israel is formed by a mighty act of redemption (Exodus 1–18). In step two, God takes his people to Mt. Sinai and proposes to them like a bridegroom proposes to a bride. God reveals himself as YHWH, and Israel is bound to God in a covenant relationship (Exodus 19–24).

Let's look at several aspects of the formation of God's people.

We see judgment against the Egyptian gods, as well as judgment against Pharaoh himself. We see the beginning of what will become a 1,500-year practice of the sacrifice of a Passover lamb. God calls Israel his treasured possession, a priestly kingdom, holy nation, with election to privilege and service. They are to be a display—showcase people for the sake of the nations.

In the latter part of Exodus, we see God coming once again to dwell with his people, this time in a portable home called a tabernacle as they make their way to the Promised Land.

THE EGYPTIAN WORLDVIEW CONFRONTED

Though the plagues in Egypt may appear arbitrary to us, they weren't random miracles. Figure 3.3 ililustrates the correlation between the Egyptian plagues and the gods that formed the Egyptian worldview.

Each plague was a demonstration to the Egyptians, and to Israel, of the superiority of YHWH over the gods of Egypt and their magical worldview. Don't miss the fact that God was intentionally turning their worldview on its head by directly attacking their pantheon of gods. The plagues climax with the killing of Pharaoh's firstborn, his successor to the throne, who was considered a deity in that day.

EGYPTIAN DEITY	PLAGUES
KHNUM – GUARDIAN OF THE NILE HAPI – SPIRIT OF THE NILE	THE NILE TURNS TO BLOOD (EX 7:19)
HEKET – GODDESS OF BIRTH, WHO MANIFEST AS A FROG	THE WATERS ARE FILLED WITH DEAD FROGS (EXOD 7:28–29; 8:1)
SEB – GOD OF THE EARTH	THE DUST OF THE LAND BECOMES LICE (EXOD 8:12–13)
AMUN-RA – CREATOR GOD, WITH THE HEAD OF A BEETLE	SWARMS OF INSECTS FILL THE AIR (EXOD 8:24)
HATHOR – GODDESS OF THE DESERT, WITH THE HEAD OF A COW APIS – GOD OF FERTILITY IN THE FORM OF A BULL	ALL THE CATTLE OF EGYPT DIE (EXOD 9:3–7)
IMHOTEP – GOD OF MEDICINE AND HEALING	BOILS BREAK OUT ON ALL OF THE EGYPTIANS (EXOD 9:9–11)
NUT – GODDESS OF THE SKY SETH – GOD OF WIND AND STORMS	HAIL DESTROYS EVERY HERB AND TREE (EXOD 9:25)
MIN – GOD OF FERTILITY	LOCUSTS EAT EVERY GREEN THING IN EGYPT (EXOD 10:15)
ATEN OR AMUN-RE – GOD OF THE SUN	THICK DARKNESS COVERS EGYPT (EXOD 10:21–23)
MESKHENET – GODDESS OF CHILDBIRTH	THE DEATH OF THE FIRSTBORN (EXOD 12:29–30)

© 2018 BibleJourney

Figure 3.3, Egyptian Deities and Plagues

GOD'S PURPOSE

God's purpose for each of the plagues comes in the form of the refrain, so that "you will know that I am the Lord your God." When we get to the New Testament, John records miracles that he calls "signs." In his Gospel, John will say, "Jesus performed many other signs in the presence of his disciples, which are not recorded in this book. But these are written that you may believe that Jesus is the Messiah, the Son of God, and that by believing you may have life in his name" (John 20:30–31).

COMMON ELEMENTS WITH ANCIENT TREATIES

Treaties in the ANE were typically between the conquering party, which is referred to as the suzerain, and the conquered party, referred to as the vassal—two unequal parties. The suzerain dictated the terms of the treaty, which typically committed protection for the vassal in exchange for loyalty and taxes from the vassal.

ANE treaties contained common elements as shown in Figure 3.4.

These primary elements are present here in Exodus and are also evident in the structure of Deuteronomy.

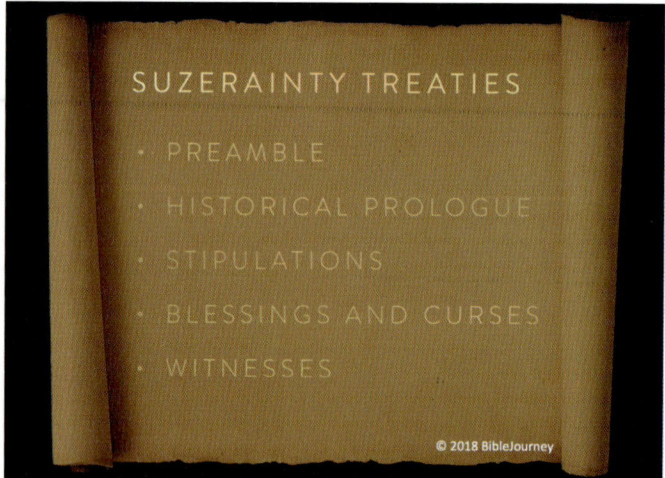

Figure 3.4, Suzerainty Treaties

Although often omitted in ANE treaties, in some cases, there is also what is referred to as the "Deposit or Tablet Clause," in which provisions are made for the deposition of the treaty in a temple and for periodic public readings of it.

EXAMPLE ANE COVENANT

Figure 3.5 is an example of an ANE covenant that traces back to the time of the Hittites.

You can find these elements in the covenants of Exodus, Deuteronomy and Joshua. In just one short sentence in Exodus, for example, God provides both the preamble and the historical prologue when he says, "I am the Lord your God who brought you out of Egypt." In other words, "I have a claim on you."

These elements also appear in modern-day covenants, such as a marriage document, a real estate deed, a will, and other legal documents.

"'You yourselves have seen what I did to Egypt, and how I carried you on eagles' wings and brought you to myself. Now if you obey me fully and keep my covenant, then out of all nations you will be my

treasured possession. Although the whole earth is mine, you will be for me a kingdom of priests and a holy nation.' These are the words you are to speak to the Israelites."

–EXODUS 19:4-7

Six Elements of an Ancient Near Eastern Covenant

Preamble: Introduced the Suzerain and justified his right to demand the vassal's allegiance: "These are the words of the Sun, Suppiluliumas, the great king. the king of the land of the Hittites, the valiant. the favorite of the Storm-god" Ex 20:2a; Dt 1 :1-5; Js 24:2

Historical Prologue: Recounts the events and/or relationship between parties leading up to the moment of entering into the covenant, often citing the benevolent actions of the suzerain and the rebellious actions of the vassal 'Previously the king of Egypt and his cronies were hostile to the Sun ... but you parted from them and joined with me.' Ex 20:2b; Dt 1:6-4:49; Js 24:2b-13

Stipulations: Specify the obligations imposed on the vassal "He who lives in peace with the Sun lives at peace with you, but he who is an enemy to the Sun is an enemy to you." (No foreign relationships allowed; Respond to call to arms; Lasting loyalty to the king). Ex 20:3ff; Dt 5-26; Js 24:14-21

Blessings and Curses: Suzerain specifies what he will do to the vassal who disobeys and what blessings he will bestow on him for obedience "May Ashur, king of the gods. decree for you an evil, unpropitious fate, and not grant you fatherhood and old age." "May Ninurta fell you with his fierce arrow, and fill the plain with your corpses, give your flesh to eagles and vultures to feed on." "May all your teeth fall out except one, and may it be abscessed." Ex 23:20-33; Dt 27-30

Deposit or Tablet Clause: Provisions were made for the deposition of the treaty in a temple and for periodic public readings of it. Often omitted an ANE. Dt 31:9-13; Js 24:26

Witnesses: Typically, a long list of gods or elements (mountains, rivers, springs, heaven and earth, sea, clouds, and the wind), who are to bring about the blessings or curses. "The treaty which he has made binding with you before Jupiter, Venus, Saturn, Mercury, Mars, and Sirius; before Ashur, Enlil, Ea and Marduk..." Dt 30:19; 31:26; Js 24:22

© 2018 BibleJourney

Figure 3.5, Six Elements of an Ancient Near Eastern Covenant

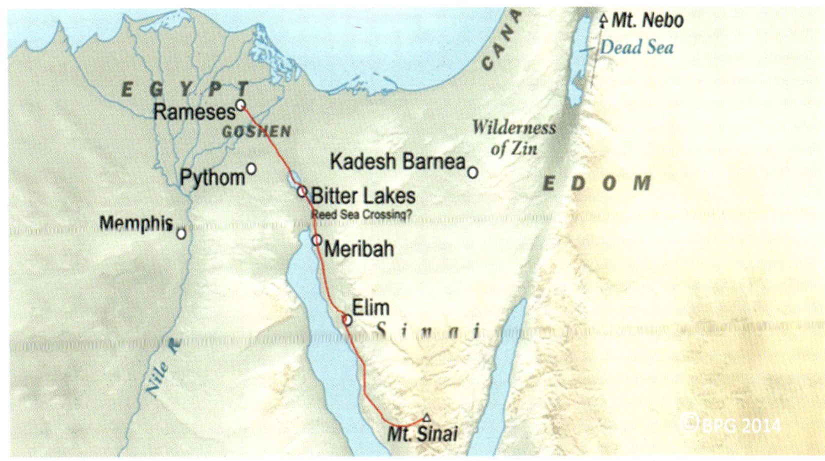

Figure 3.6, Exodus Route: Part 1

EXODUS ROUTE

Once the Israelites crossed through the Sea of Reeds, perhaps at the Bitter Lakes, they went into the Sinai. There are different routes that have been proposed for where they went next and where Mt. Sinai is located. The traditional place for Mt. Sinai is shown in Figure 3.6 at the lower end of the Sinai Peninsula.

MT. SINAI

Figure 3.7 is a view atop Mt. Sinai, a spot like the one where Moses and probably Elijah had stayed while they had their divine encounters. Imagine the gravity of an encounter with God in a place like this.

Figure 3.7, Mt. Sinai

LEVITICUS: LIVING WITH A HOLY GOD

If we had to choose one word to describe the book of Leviticus, it would undoubtedly be "sacred," or "holy," which means *set apart for God*. The Israelites are instructed on sacred space, sacred offerings, sacred personnel, a sacred community and sacred time.

Figure 3.8, The Tabernacle

SACRED SPACE

This 1:1 scale model of the original Tabernacle is near Eilat in the southernmost part of Israel.

The Holy Place is the tent-like structure. Inside the Holy Place was the Holy of Holies, which contained the Ark of the Covenant. There was a courtyard around the Holy Place, which was dangerous for anyone other than the priests. It included the altar of sacrifice and the laver for washing prior to entry into the Holy Place. Outside of that space was Israel's camp, which was holy. So when the Israelites dealt with things that were unclean, they were instructed to set them outside the camp.

ARK OF THE COVENANT

The cherubim over the ark represented the presence of God in the Tabernacle, and the Ark contained three things: manna, Aaron's budding staff, and the tablets (Exodus 25:17–22).

Figure 3.9, The Ark of the Covenant

SACRED OFFERINGS

An offering is a gift brought to God. Leviticus provides a system of offerings that were performed by priests on behalf of people. Different offerings were required for different sin offenses. The purpose of each of the offerings was to restore an individual's relationship with God. The system of sacred offerings was a temporary system which pointed forward to the ultimate sacrifice of Jesus on the cross, the once and for all atonement for the sins of mankind.

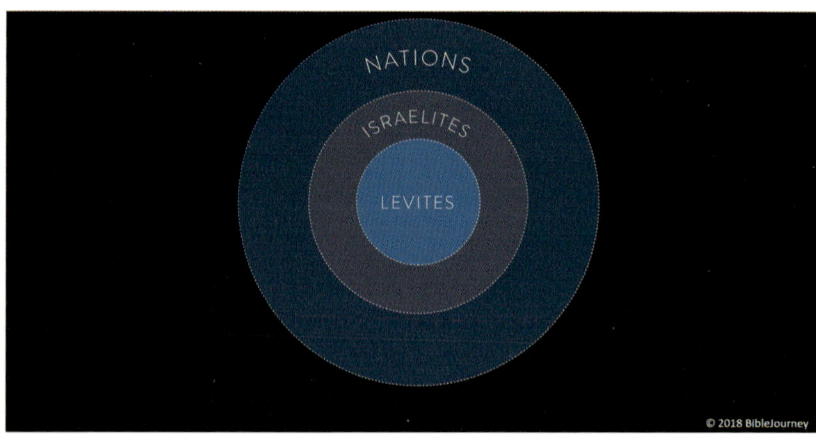

Figure 3.10, Sacred Personnel

SACRED PERSONNEL

The Levites represented the firstborn of all Israelites. The Israelites, in turn, represented the firstfruits of all nations.

EPHOD

As a reminder of the priests' role as mediators for God's people, they wore the names and emblems of the tribes of Israel on their shoulders and across their hearts on a breastplate, which was called an ephod (Exodus 28:12).

Figure 3.11, Priest's Ephod

SACRED COMMUNITY

The nation of Israel was to be God's treasured possession among all peoples, a kingdom of priests and a holy nation (Exodus 19:5-6). They were to be set apart from the other nations as holy to God, chosen from all the nations to be God's own special treasure (Leviticus 20:26, Deuteronomy 14:2). They were to be a light to the world, so that the Gentile nations would be drawn to become members of God's family, and that God's salvation would reach the ends of the earth (Isaiah 49:6).

SACRED TIME

With respect to sacred time, the Israelites were instructed to observe feasts or festivals, in remembrance and honor of God. These pilgrimage holidays correlated with the agricultural cycle, and they were reminders to express their faith in the God of both history and agriculture.

PILGRIMAGE HOLIDAYS			
HOLIDAYS	AGRICULTURE	HISTORY	PROPHECY
PASSOVER *(PESACH)*	OMER	EXODUS	PASSOVER LAMB
PENTECOST *(SHAVUOT)*	FIRST FRUITS	SINAI	PENTECOST
TABERNACLES *(SUKKOT)*	INGATHERING	BOOTHS	HEAVEN

© 2018 BibleJourney

Figure 3.12, Pilgrimage Holidays

Passover, or Pesach, took place at the beginning of the barley harvest. They entered the Temple and waved an omer of barley, thanking God and remembering the Passover that took place prior to their Exodus from Egypt. The Feast of Passover pointed forward to the ultimate Passover sacrifice of Christ 1,500 years later.

Pentecost, or Shavuot, took place 50 days later, at the beginning of the wheat harvest, offering the firstfruits and recalling the giving of the covenant on Mt. Sinai. This Feast of Pentecost pointed forward to the giving of the Spirit on the day of Pentecost in Acts.

Tabernacles, or Sukkot, took place at the time of the ingathering of the fruit harvest, and recalls the time God provided for the Israelites when they lived in booths in the wilderness. The Feast of Tabernacles continues to point forward to our eventual dwelling with Christ in the heavenly realm.

So each of these major feast days had a correlation with both history and the agricultural cycle.

NUMBERS: JOURNEYING TO THE LAND

In the book of Numbers, we see God's provision, protection and guidance as their shepherd during their journey.

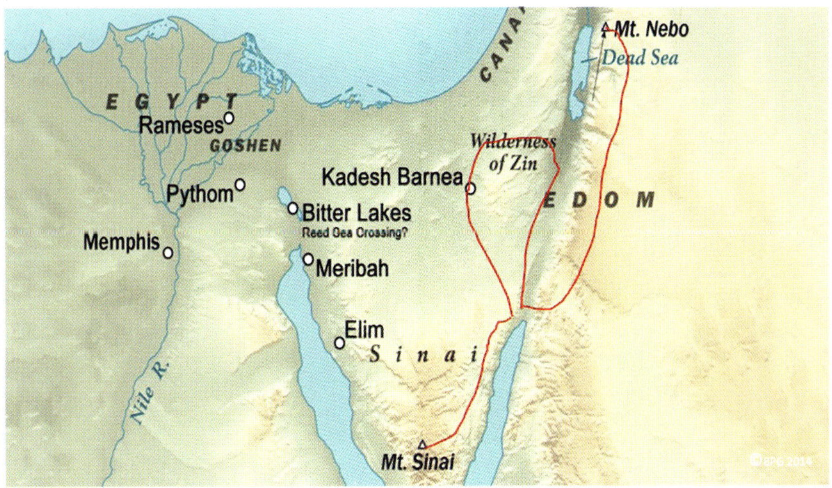

Figure 3.13, Exodus Route: Part 2

Figure 3.13 shows the route of the Israelites as they made their way from Mt. Sinai to Mt. Nebo, the place of Moses' death prior to the Israelites entering the Promised Land. Because of Israel's disobedience and lack of faith, they wandered for 40 years in the wilderness. An entire generation died off before the people were allowed to enter the Promised Land.

During their wilderness sojourn, Israel lived in temporary shelters or booths like the one in Figure 3.14.

Figure 3.14, Wilderness Booth

Figure 3.15 is a picture of a luxurious booth in Jerusalem, in which they would feast with the best of tableware and linens.

Figure 3.15, Modern Booth

DEUTERONOMY: ON THE BORDERS OF THE LAND

In the last book of the Torah, Deuteronomy, we see three sermons from Moses as he instructs the people to remain faithful to the covenant:

- Sermon One: God's faithfulness to Israel (1:6–4:40)
- Sermon Two: God's covenant law (4:44–28)
- Sermon Three: Options for the future (29–30)

After reminding the people of God's faithfulness and the covenant into which they entered, Moses lays out the two paths from which to choose, as well as the blessings from following the correct path and the curses from following the wrong path.

SCENE TWO: A LAND FOR HIS PEOPLE

JOSHUA: THE CONQUEST OF THE LAND

Moses' disobedience at Kadesh in Numbers 20 prevented him from bringing the Israelites into the Promised Land. That task was left for Joshua, his successor.

Israel's entry into the Promised Land marks the beginning of what is referred to as the Historical Period, which goes through the book of Esther. The Historical Period explores the Mission of the People of God in the Promised Land. Although we won't go through the details of the conquest itself, let's consider the land and its significance.

SIGNIFICANCE OF THE LAND

Figure 3.16 is a *geographical* picture that is taken from space.

The small circle is the traditional place for Mt. Sinai, where Israel received its covenant. The Promised Land is the large oval, with the Sea of Galilee at the top and the Dead Sea below it. The Rift Valley

Figure 3.16, Mt. Sinai and the Promised Land

follows the Jordan River which flows into the Sea of Galilee and continues down to the Dead Sea, and then the Rift Valley goes all the way down to eastern Africa.

The Rift Valley creates a natural boundary on what was originally meant to be the eastern boundary of the Promised Land, until some of the tribes negotiated to stay east of it. There are mountains which are about 3,000 feet above sea level on the western side and about 5,000 feet above sea level on the eastern side.

Israel entered the Promised Land from the eastern side.

GEOGRAPHICAL ZONES

Figure 3.17 is a cross-sectional view of the five major geographic zones of the Promised Land.

The Coastal Plain is flat and open and is the most obvious way of international travel north and south. The Shephelah consists of low hills with terraced agriculture. It was the disputed territory between the international coast and the hills. The Hill Country *west* of the

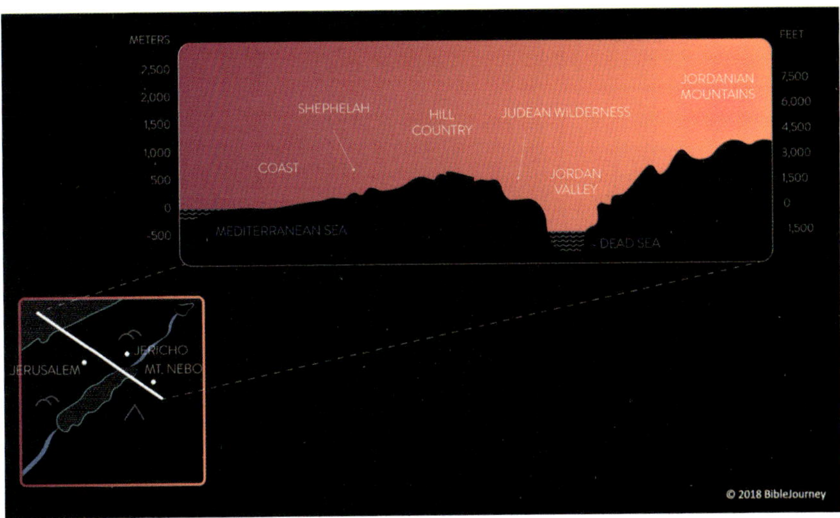

Figure 3.17, Geographical Zones of the Promised Land

Jordan River comprises the primary territories of Judah and Israel, and includes the Judean wilderness. The Jordan River Valley is part of the Rift Valley that runs through the Red Sea and East Africa. The Hill Country east of the Jordan River is known as *the Transjordan*; it is home to ancient Ammon, Moab and Edom.

With respect to the climate, the wind off the Mediterranean Sea picks up moisture and drops rain on the hills on both sides of the Jordan River.

TRIBAL ALLOTMENTS

Figure 3.18 is the map you will find in the back of most Bibles. It shows the tribal allotments discussed in Joshua 13–21.

Notice that two and a half tribes will settle on the east side of the Jordan Valley (Joshua 1:10–18) as a result of an agreement made with Moses in Numbers 32:1–5.

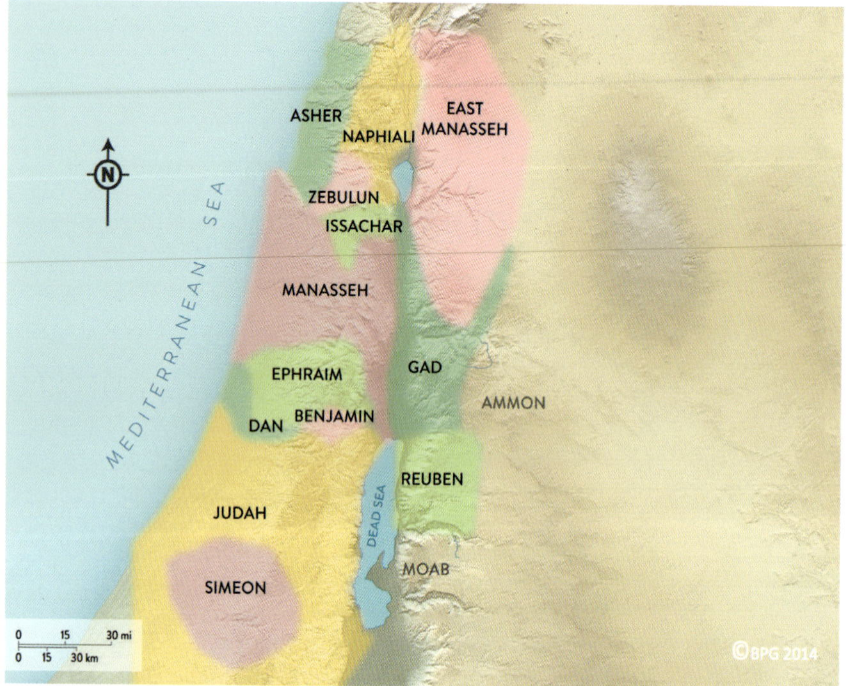

Figure 3.18, Tribal Allotments

THE GREAT TEMPTATIONS

There are two aspects of the land that led to what we call in Bible Journey the "Two Great Temptations" of Israel:

- The Great Temptation of Peace
- The Great Temptation of Prosperity

THE GREAT TEMPTATION OF PEACE

The "Land Between" the great empires of Egypt and Mesopotamia was rarely independent. Over time, a number of empires cast their shadow over this land.

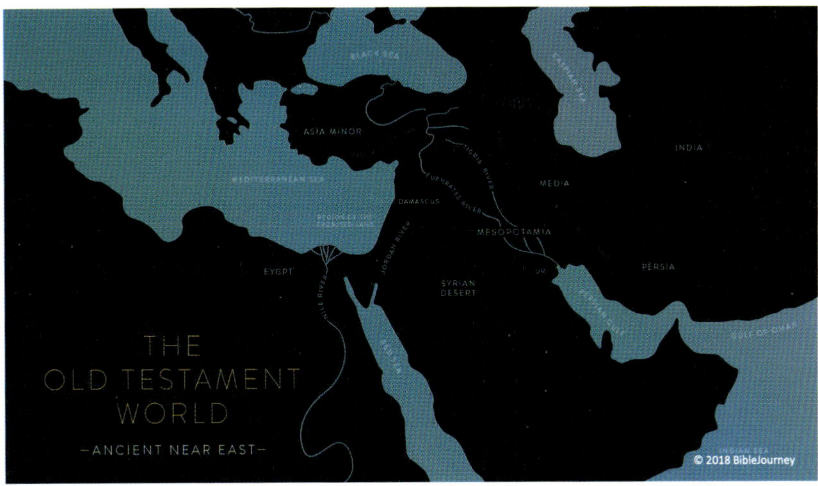

Figure 3.19, The "Land Between"

THE LAND "IN THE WAY"

In Figure 3.20, close-up of the Promised Land, you can see how it falls directly along the international highway from Egypt to Mesopotamia.

Figure 3.20, The International Highway

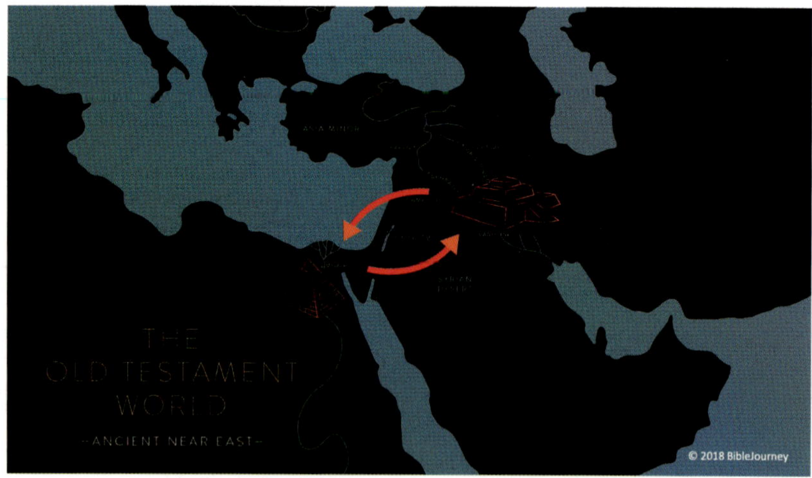

Figure 3.21, Empire-building Hydraulic Civilizations

It was essentially "in the way," or "on the way" of conquering kings as they expanded their empires.

Empire-building "hydraulic" civilizations emerged at both ends of the Fertile Crescent between 3500–3200 BC (Figure 3.21). The earliest civilizations were spurred on by the mighty rivers of Egypt's Nile on one end and the Tigris and Euphrates on the other end. Within 100–200 years there were massive buildings with detailed religious meaning *(pyramids and ziggurats)*, social complexity *(kings and nobles, priests and temples and slaves)* and language *(cuneiform in Mesopotamia, hieroglyphics in Egypt)*. Along with a stable water supply, language and writing provided the tools to manage the environment and the blossoming cultures.

THE EGYPTIAN EMPIRE

One of the first global empires was Egypt, pictured in Figure 3.22, when Israel was in slavery in Egypt *(New Kingdom: ~1500–1200 BC)*.

The empire spread south to Nubia and all along the Fertile Crescent north into Mesopotamia.

Figure 3.22, The Egyptian Empire

Figure 3.23, Cloverleaf Map of the World

The "Cloverleaf Map of the World," Figure 3.23, designed in Germany in the 1500s, shows Jerusalem at the center of Europe, Africa and Asia.

Although not accurate from a purely geographical point of view, it perfectly captures the way in which the Promised Land was "in the way" and "on the way" between the great empires of the ancient world. Israel was positioned at this crossroads to be a witness to the unique claims of YHWH, who was not only their God, but the God of all creation and all nations. However, this placement led to what we call in Bible Journey one of the two "Great Temptations," the Great Temptation of Peace *(Great Temptation #1).*

Israel was put in a place where they would have to decide about who they would trust for safety. Although God asked for their loyalty to him alone, Israel was thus tempted to reach out to its neighbors to make political alliances for its safety.

So the *location* of Israel led to the Great Temptation of Peace.

THE GREAT TEMPTATION OF PROSPERITY

In seeking prosperity, Israel "hedged its bets" by integrating the worship of gods other than Yahweh. This practice is known as syncretism, which is more generally defined as the mixing of two religious, philosophical or cultural systems. Since Israel was an agricultural society heavily dependent upon the proper amount of rain, the people mixed the worship of Baal, the storm god, with the worship of Yahweh, with the hope that Baal would provide the needed rains to ensure a prosperous crop.

Figure 3.24, Satellite View of the Nile
Image Courtesy of NASA
and Visible Earth

The satellite image of Figure 3.24 gives you a great view of the Nile River.[22]

The narrow green band is the highly fertile area where the Nile annually overflows and spills its rich minerals into the soil. The Nile is surrounded by an arid desert. The narrow green band might look insignificant from a satellite, but

22 Visible Earth, accessed November 24, 2023, https://visibleearth.nasa.gov/images/71790/the-nile-egypt.

Egypt today is a significant supplier of agricultural products to other nations.

The Israelites lived in the highly fertile delta region up north along the coast of the Mediterranean Sea, so they enjoyed the ease in which they were able to grow crops. In Deuteronomy 11, Moses described the Promised Land to God's people and said it would not be like Egypt with its river and its irrigation that could be done by foot.

Figure 3.25 is a picture taken along the Nile of a farmer opening an irrigation channel by moving mud with his foot.

This gives you a sense of how rich the soil is along the Nile, which Moses places in contrast to what the Israelites will face in the Promised Land.

Figure 3.25, Nile Irrigation by Foot

THE AGRICULTURAL CYCLE

The Promised Land shares the two-season climate of the Eastern Mediterranean—a dry summer with rainless months, and a wet season initiated by "early rains" and ending with "latter rains."

Recall that the pilgrimage festivals celebrated certain agricultural realities. Passover marked the onset of the grain harvest with the first sheaf of barley in the spring. Pentecost celebrated the beginning of

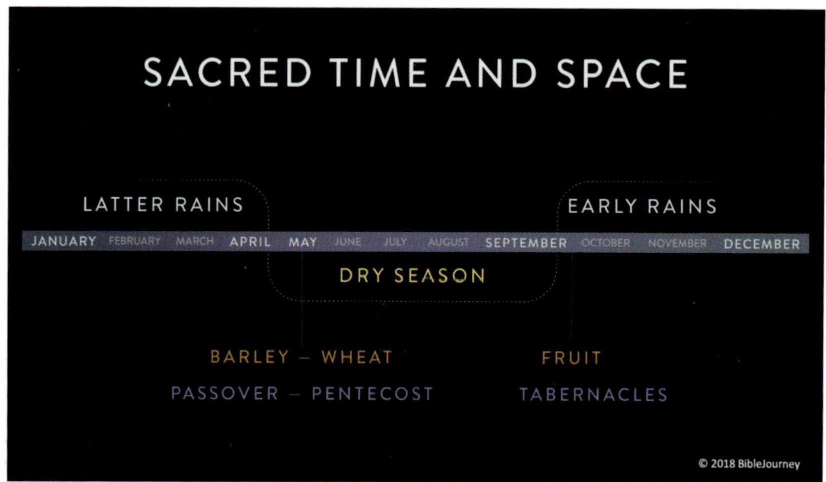

Figure 3.26, Sacred Time and Space

the full grain harvest with both barley and wheat, following the seven weeks of climatic uncertainty. The Feast of Tabernacles in the fall was also called the Feast of Ingathering because it coincided with the fruit harvest.

SIGNIFICANCE OF RAINFALL

Figure 3.27 shows the average rainfall of the Promised Land.

The rainfall varies from approximately 52 inches per year in the north near Mt. Hermon, down to 0 inches near Beersheba, below which is the desert region of the Negev. This is why you will hear the Promised Land referred to as "Dan to Beersheba," which is essentially the inhabited area of Israel.

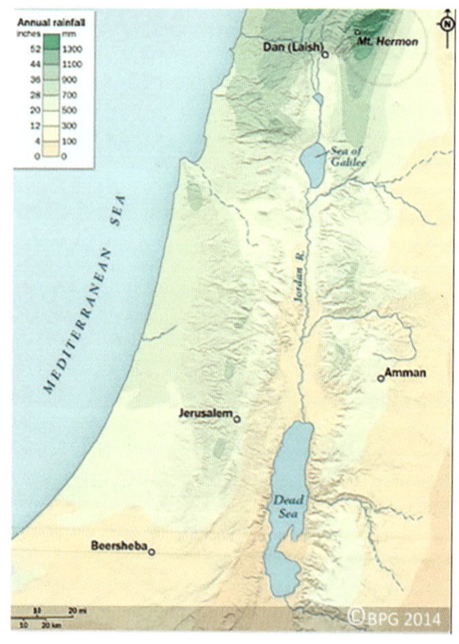

Figure 3.27, Rainfall in the Promised Land

The people depended on the Lord for the early rains and the latter rains. So, the *rainfall* tells us a lot about Israel's journey of faith and its religious choices, and it led to the other Great Temptation, the Great Temptation of Prosperity *(Great Temptation #2).*

BAAL, THE STORM GOD

In addition to worshiping YHWH, the Israelites worshiped Baal, the storm god, who was a constant contender for Israel's trust and loyalty, because he was associated with the forces of nature that produced rainfall.

He was often portrayed as a bull or riding on a bull with a lightning bolt in his hand. Baal was a Canaanite fertility deity.

Figure 3.28, Baal, the Storm God

JUDGES: FAILURE TO BE A DISPLAY PEOPLE

The story continues in the book of Judges, in which the Israelites fail to fully take the Promised Land as directed by God.

THE CYCLE

Judges shows us the cycles of judgment that follow.

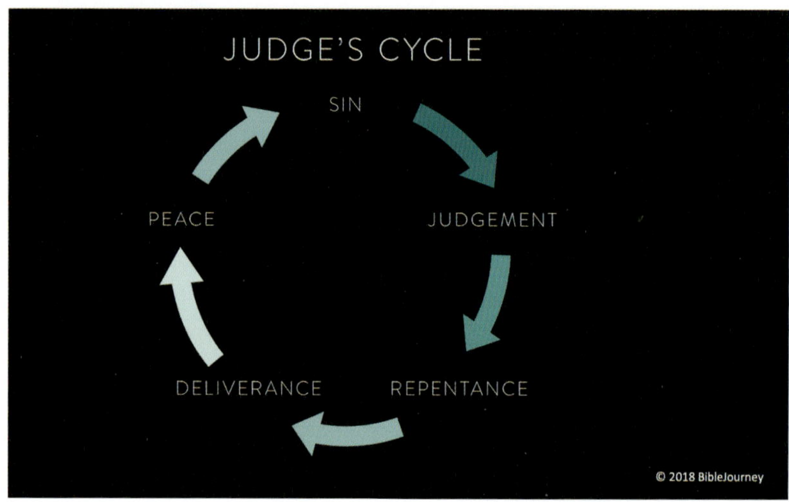

Figure 3.29, The Cycle of Judges

This cycle repeats throughout the book of Judges. It starts with a period of peace, and then moves to rebellion or sin, judgment on the nation, repentance, deliverance and then another period of peace.

THE SPIRAL

Judges is not just a cycle. It is a downward spiral.

The refrain in Judges is, "In those days there was no king in Israel. Everyone did what was right in his own eyes."

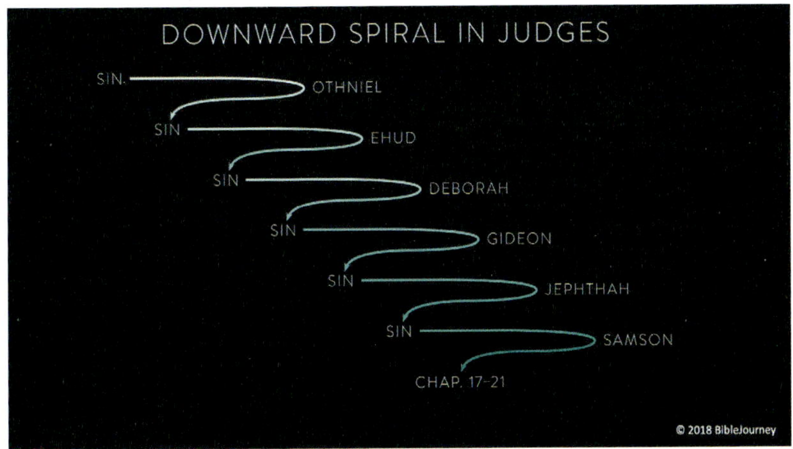

Figure 3.30, The Downward Spiral in Judges

THE CYCLE: ANOTHER VIEW

Figure 3.31 is another way to view the cycle that shows up in the book of Judges.

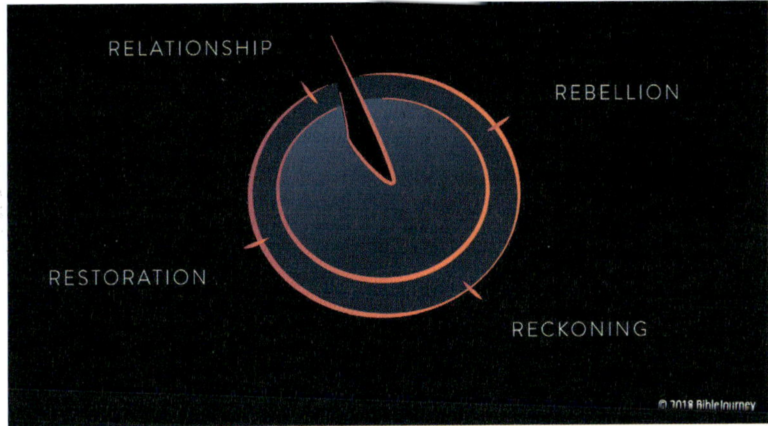

Figure 3.31, The Cycle: Another View

If we're honest with ourselves, we would likely recognize this as the cycle of our own individual lives, during which we drift away or even rebel against God, then face the consequences or the reckoning, after which we cry out to God for forgiveness and are restored into his grace once again following our repentance. Don't miss the fact that our relationship with God always starts with God's grace! It is a free gift, not something we deserve, or we have to earn. God is the faithful covenant partner in this relationship.

THE KINGS

Revisiting our timeline, as we come out of the period of the Judges, we've completed the period of the Conquest and Settlement, and we're about to enter the period of the kings. So, we are at approximately 1000 BC.

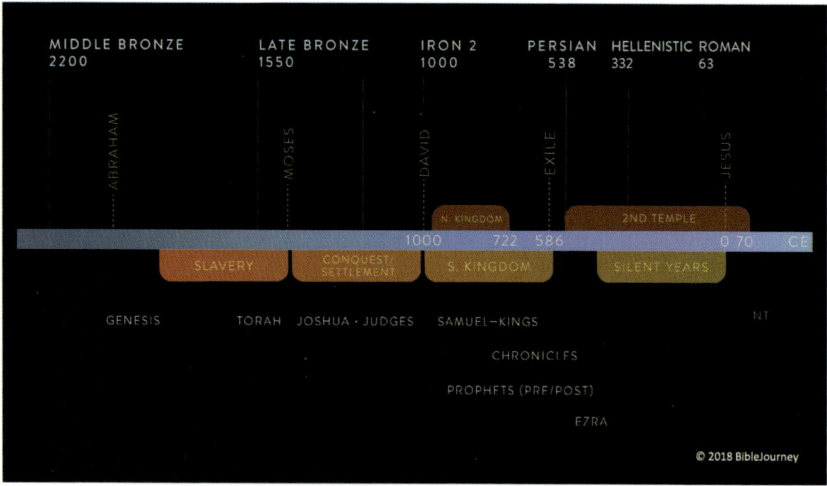

Figure 3.32, Timeline of the Bible

SAMUEL: ISRAEL TRANSFORMED INTO A KINGDOM

The people were supposed to look to God as their king. Recognizing that the people would fail in this regard, earlier in the story, Moses told the people in Deuteronomy that when they ask for a king, they were to have a king that met certain criteria.

"When you enter the land the Lord your God is giving you and have taken possession of it and settled in it, and you say, 'Let us set a king over us like all the nations around us,' be sure to appoint over you a king the Lord your God chooses. He must be from among your fellow Israelites. Do not place a foreigner over you, one who is not an Israelite. The king, moreover, must not acquire great numbers of horses for himself or make the people return to Egypt to get more of them, for the Lord has told you, 'You are not to go back that way again.' He must not take many wives, or his heart will be led astray. He must not accumulate large amounts of silver and gold.

When he takes the throne of his kingdom, he is to write for himself on a scroll a copy of this law, taken from that of the Levitical priests. It is to be with him, and he is to read it all the days of his life so that he may learn to revere the Lord his God and follow carefully all the words of this law and these decrees and not consider himself better than his fellow Israelites and turn from the law to the right or to the left. Then he and his descendants will reign a long time over his kingdom in Israel."

DEUTERONOMY 17:14–20

1 Samuel tells us the story of Saul, the first king, who fails on several fronts.

DAVIDIC COVENANT

King David follows, and the new element in the covenant with David is the idea of a kingdom that will rule forever. David is remembered as Israel's greatest king, but he also has his failures. In spite of David's failures, God promises a Davidic offspring who will rule forever.

KINGS: COVENANT FAILURE

David's son, Solomon, requests and receives wisdom from God. Solomon built the first Temple in ~970 BC, a Temple which includes elements that reflect back on the Garden of Eden, God's first dwelling place with mankind on Earth. After Solomon's reign, the kingdom was split in two.

GOD'S JUDGMENT

- 722 BC: Israel is deported by Assyria
- 586 BC: Judah is exiled by Babylon

Despite warnings from the Prophets, Israel's covenant failure continues and ends in destruction and exile. The Northern Kingdom of Israel was ransacked by God's instrument of justice, the nation of Assyria, and a remnant was deported in 722 BC. The Southern Kingdom of Judah started to be destroyed by Assyria less than a century later, and Judah was eventually fully crushed by another of God's instruments of justice, Babylon, in 586 BC. The Temple was destroyed, and a remnant of the Southern Kingdom was taken to Babylon.

Within this story, however, we see a note of hope: Jehoiachin, one of David's descendants, is released.

THE NEO-ASSYRIAN EMPIRE

Figure 3.33 captures the extent of the Assyrian kingdom in 650 BC, after the Northern Kingdom of Israel was taken into exile.

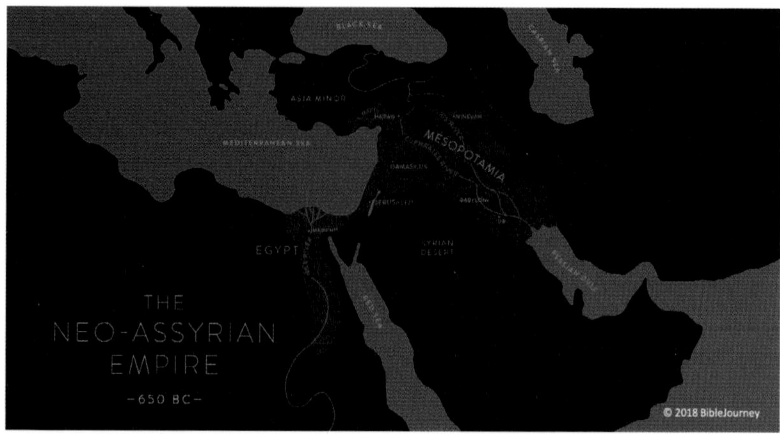

Figure 3.33, The Neo-Assyrian Empire

Notice how deep into Egypt the Assyrians went. Global domination in the Fertile Crescent always moved to control the civilizations on both ends.

THE NEO-BABYLONIAN EMPIRE

The Neo-Babylonian Empire took over the Assyrian Empire and extended it further in all directions. Figure 3.35 shows the world of Judah's exile in 600 B.C.

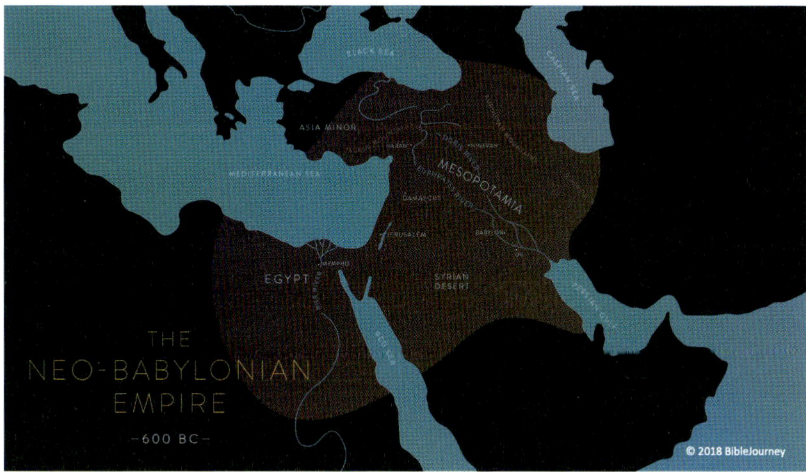

Figure 3.34, The Neo-Babylonian Empire

THE PERSIAN EMPIRE

The Persian Empire took over the Babylonians and extended the borders even further. As shown in Figure 3.35, in 500 BC, they ruled parts of Europe, Northeast Africa and even India.

The Persians created a true empire—a road system that connected the parts of the world, a postal system and a universal language

Figure 3.35, The Persian Empire

EZRA AND NEHEMIAH: ISRAEL RETURNS TO THE LAND

In 539 BC, King Cyrus of Persia conquered the Babylonians and allowed Israel to return to the Promised Land. Zerubbabel rebuilt the Temple, Ezra reformed the people, and Nehemiah rebuilt the city walls.

So, the Israelite remnant regained its land and rebuilt the Temple, but there was no Davidic king on the throne. Before we continue on the timeline into the Intertestamental Period, let's take a look at the Prophets of the Historical Period.

THE PROPHETS

The prophetic writings don't give us new history; instead, the Prophets *interpret* the Historical Period for us. Prophets were spokespersons for God who called people into a covenant relationship and usually delivered a twofold message of warning and hope.

Some key prophetic messages include the fact that God's purpose will prevail, a new covenant and kingdom will come through a Messiah, Israel will be gathered and purified, and nations will be drawn to Israel.

THE FOUR "I'S"

We talked about the two Great Temptations, which led to two significant ways in which Israel failed to keep its covenant with God. Figure 3.36 shows you all four basic ways in which the Israelites failed to remain faithful, which are the *same* four basic ways we sin today.

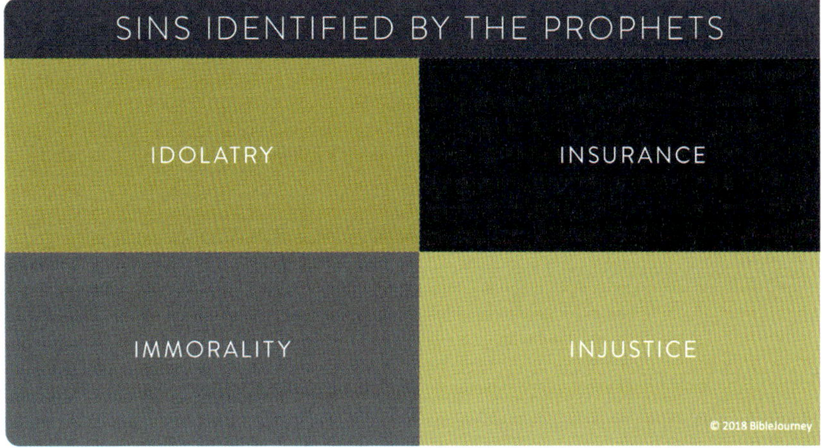

Figure 3.36, Sins Identified by the Prophets

In Bible Journey, we call these the four "I's":

- Idolatry (the worship of things other than God)
- Insurance (the alliances we form rather than trusting in God alone)
- Immorality
- Injustice

These are the four categories you will hear about when we superimpose the messages of the Prophets over the historical record of Israel.

TERMS AND TIMELINE

The Prophets are referred to with many terms, such as *Former Prophets and Latter Prophets, Major Prophets and Minor Prophets, Classical Prophets and Pre-classical Prophets*, and other terms.

The Latter Prophets are prophets who have books in their names in the Bible and are sometimes called the Writing Prophets. They prophesied during the time period that correlates with the kings and carried into the Exile and the Post-Exilic period, finishing with Malachi, the last prophet of the Old Testament.

So, these so-called Latter Prophets, or Writing Prophets, wrote from approximately 1000 BC to approximately 430 BC, after which we have a period of about 400 years, sometimes referred to as the "Silent Years," during which there was no recorded prophesy until John the Baptist came on the scene.

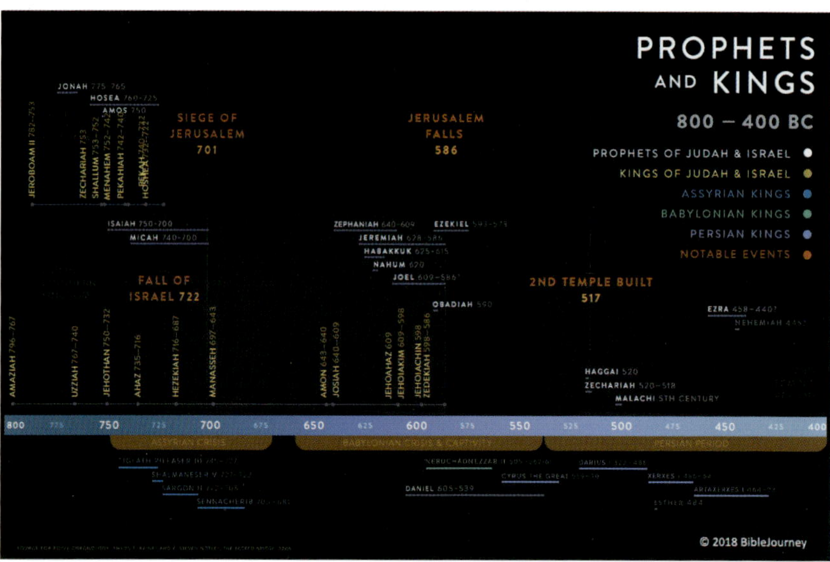

Figure 3.37, Timeline of the Prophets and Kings

ACT 3 KEY TAKEAWAYS

- Following two additional catastrophic episodes, the Flood and the Tower of Babel, God chooses Abraham and establishes a covenant with him to continue his plan for mankind.
- Covenant promises: Abraham's descendants will become a great nation; they will possess the Promised Land; and they will be a light and a blessing to the other nations.
- The promise continues through the patriarchs.
- God rescues his people from oppression in Egypt and brings them to Mt. Sinai, where he proposes to them in his covenant with Moses and instructs them in the Law.
- God once again dwells with his people, this time in a temporary dwelling—the Tabernacle.
- God makes a covenant with David, and David unites the kingdom, and brings the Ark to Jerusalem.
- David's son, Solomon, builds the Temple on Mount Zion.
- The kingdom splits into Israel (Northern Kingdom) and Judah (Southern Kingdom).
- The people fail to fulfill their mission, the land is devastated and the Temple is destroyed, and God exiles his people through his chosen instruments, Assyria (Israel in 722 BC) and Babylon (Judah in 586 BC).
- The people return to the land 70 years later, and they rebuild the Temple and reinitiate the sacrificial system, but without a Davidic king.
- Prophets overlay messages of warning and hope during the historical books.

ACT 3 CHALLENGE QUESTION

What sin is preventing you from having the full relationship you desire with God?

ADDITIONAL REFLECTION QUESTIONS

- What did you find surprising about this part of the Bible story?
- What else did you find interesting about this part of the Bible story?
- How has this part of the Bible story challenged your thinking?
- How has this part of the Bible story shaped your worldview?
- What will you do differently as a result of what you learned?
- Who will you tell about what you have learned?

Chapter 4

INTERLUDE: BETWEEN THE TESTAMENTS *(KINGDOM STORY WAITS FOR AN ENDING)*

The Intertestamental Period is the time between the last book of the Old Testament, Malachi, and the Gospels. This is the period in which God was preparing the world for sending his Son.

Let's take a look at some highlights of this 400-year period.

> ***"The Intertestamental Period bridges the testaments through the preparation for the Gospel."***
>
> –Dr. Robert Cooley[23]

HISTORICAL OVERVIEW

Our focus on the Intertestamental Period will be on the significance of the period in preparation for the Gospel.

23 Robert E Cooley, Adult Education notes, 2006.

HELLENISTIC INFLUENCE

Perhaps the greatest influence during this period was Alexander the Great, who brought the Greek, or Hellenistic, culture and opened the Jewish mind to other ideas.

SIGNIFICANT EVENTS

Two significant events of this period include (1) the desecration of the Temple by Antiochus IV, in 167 BC, and (2) the cleansing of the Temple by Judas Maccabeus, in 164 BC, from which we celebrate the Feast of Hanukkah.

EMERGENCE OF SYNAGOGUES

During this period, synagogues provided the means through which the Jews maintained their cultural distinctiveness, with worship, prayer and study of the Scriptures.

FIVE FUNDAMENTAL BELIEFS

Throughout the Intertestamental Period, the Jews held on to five fundamental beliefs. First, they believed in monotheism—that there was only one God, who was Creator of the world and Ruler of history. Second, God had elected, or chosen, Israel for a special purpose in the Abrahamic covenant. Third, God had given Israel the Torah to direct its way of life. Fourth, the land was holy because God dwelled with Israel in the Temple. Fifth, God would complete his redemptive work.

GROWING TENSIONS

However, tensions grew between the Hellenistic pagan influence and faithfulness to the Torah, and as a result, hatred intensified toward the Gentile oppressors and the compromising Jews.

JEWISH REACTIONS

Differing views emerged regarding how, when, through whom, and how to live, resulting in the emergence of five major groups:

1) The Pharisees (teachers of the Law and the oral tradition)
2) The Sadducees and priests, who compromised with the Romans and were the official teachers of the Law who opposed the oral tradition of the Pharisees, and who were the recognized representatives of mainline Jewish religion
3) The Essenes, who chose a path of withdrawal
4) The Zealots, who chose a path of violence
5) The common people, who were content to go about everyday life and wait in hope

THE PERFECT TIME

Galatians 4:4 tells us that God sent his Son into the world in his perfect timing. Let's take a look at five aspects of the first century that made it suitable for God to send his Son.

First, the world of ideas was dynamic because Alexander the Great broke down the power of tradition and opened up minds to think new thoughts and make new discoveries, particularly the discovery of the individual.

Second, Jewish society had become diverse with the emergence of these major groups.

Third, in the Pax Romana, Roman rule and law united diverse countries into one economic union, and Roman roads and security allowed for commerce and travel, so people and ideas could move, including missionaries bringing the Gospel out from Jerusalem.

Fourth, the Jewish Diaspora provided Paul with synagogues in strategic Jewish cities in which he could provide the good news in an historical Jewish context, starting with Abraham, Isaac and Jacob, and then telling the people about the one who fulfilled all the aspirations of these people, Jesus.

Fifth, the pagan influence led to moral decay, so the world was in need of a righteous Savior.

So, although we don't have any canonical, or biblical writings during this time period, God was clearly at work preparing the world for the arrival of his Son.

GOING DEEPER

For further background on the Intertestamental Period, refer to Appendix A.

INTERTESTAMENTAL PERIOD KEY TAKEAWAYS

- The 400 "Silent Years"–no prophetic writings between Malachi (~430 BC) and the New Testament.
- The Perfect Time:
    - o The world of ideas had become dynamic under Alexander the Great.
    - o Jewish society is divided into parties and sects.
    - o Pax Romana: Roman rule united diverse countries into one economic union.
    - o The Jewish Diaspora led to dispersed Jewish communities to which Paul preached from a Jewish context (Jesus as the fulfillment of the Old Testament promises).
    - o Pagan influence led to moral bankruptcy and decay—the world needed a righteous Savior.

INTERLUDE CHALLENGE QUESTION

When God is silent in your prayer life, how do you respond?

ADDITIONAL REFLECTION QUESTIONS

- What did you find surprising about this part of the Bible story?
- What else did you find interesting about this part of the Bible story?
- How has this part of the Bible story challenged your thinking?
- How has this part of the Bible story shaped your worldview?
- What will you do differently as a result of what you learned?
- Who will you tell about what you have learned?

Chapter 5

ACT 4 REDEMPTION ACCOMPLISHED: THE COMING OF THE KING

In Act 4, the Gospels, the long-awaited hero, Jesus Christ, fulfills God's promise to redeem the fallen world. The hero enters the scene.

"But when the set time had fully come, God sent his Son, born of a woman, born under the law, to redeem those under the law, that we might receive adoption to sonship."
–Galatians 4:4-5

We'll look at the life of Jesus as it progresses from his preparation for ministry to his public mission and his kingdom mission. Then we'll look at the Passion Week in Jerusalem, and finally, his commissioning of his disciples.

TIMELINE

The date of birth of Jesus is not stated in the Gospels or in any historical sources, but most biblical scholars generally accept a date of the birth between 6 BC and 4 BC, the year in which King Herod died. Jesus was taken to Egypt by his parents in order to escape the killing of the babies by King Herod. After returning to Jerusalem, Jesus was

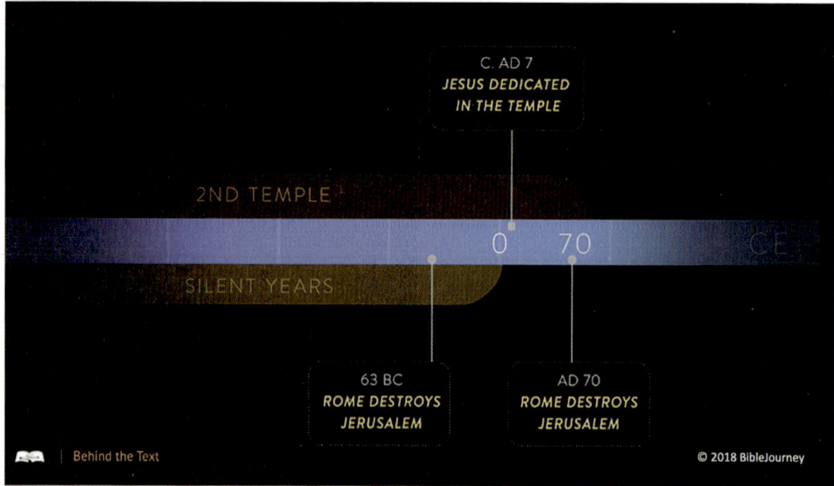

Figure 5.1, Timeline of Jesus' Early Years

dedicated in the Temple. Very little else has been documented regarding Jesus' early years. In approximately 30 AD, John the Baptist announced the arrival of the king and baptized Jesus in the Jordan River, at which time the Spirit descended upon Jesus. Jesus was then tempted three times by the Devil before embarking on his mission.

HUMBLE BEGINNING

Figure 5.2, Shepherd Field

Jesus' birth took place in the shepherds' fields like the field in Figure 5.2 outside of Jerusalem.

Despite his royal status as King of kings and Lord of lords, Jesus' life began amongst the humble and lowly shepherds who guarded the flocks to be used as sacrifices in the Temple.

JOURNEY TO EGYPT

Figure 5.3, Journey to Egypt

In Figure 5.3 you can get a sense of the journey of Jesus and his parents to Egypt. Travel on foot to Egypt is estimated to have taken approximately a week in Jesus' day.

THE WILDERNESS

Figure 5.4 will give you a sense of the wilderness in which John the Baptist lived.

Figure 5.4, Judean Wilderness

The deserts were a traditional home for prophets since the days of Elijah and Elisha, and even before them, Moses. This was the region of the Essenes, who shared with Jesus' followers an anticipation of a Second Exodus beginning in the desert (Isaiah 40:3).

JESUS' BAPTISM

Figure 5.5, Jordan River Baptism

Figure 5.5 is a modern-day image of the traditional site of the baptism of Jesus.

Baptism seems to emerge out of the notion that through some kind of ritual involving water, people can be purified. Baptism in the time of Jesus took on a special meaning, especially the baptism of John, because it referred to a form of discipleship. It was the baptism of repentance. John didn't want to baptize Jesus because he was already a righteous person; however, Jesus went through this rite of passage to identify himself with other humans who need this. As an authentication by heaven, the Holy Spirit descended like a dove, along with a voice from heaven saying, "You are my Son, whom I love; with you I am well pleased" (Luke 3:22). Jesus was given divine authority.

JESUS' TEMPTATION

Jesus went from his baptism, led by the Spirit out into the desert. Figure 5.6 shows the most likely place for Jesus to have gone from the baptismal site up into the desert to a high mountain where he was challenged by the Devil to turn stones into bread and to throw himself down.

Figure 5.6, Traditional Site of the Mount of Temptation

Jesus quoted from Deuteronomy 6 and 8, connecting Israel with himself. Jesus lived the story of Israel by going to Egypt and then leaving Egypt and crossing the Jordan, taking the lessons of the desert into the Promised Land so that from that point forward they would learn to trust Yahweh and him alone. In Deuteronomy 6 and 8, God gave Israel the spiritual fortitude to face temptation. However, unlike Israel, which succumbed to the temptations, Jesus, fasting 40 days and 40 nights, clung to the Word of God.

JESUS' PUBLIC MISSION

Jesus' ministry centered in Galilee, and also included Judea and the more remote areas of Samaria and Phoenicia. Judea is near the Dead Sea. Samaria is a land between Galilee and Judea.

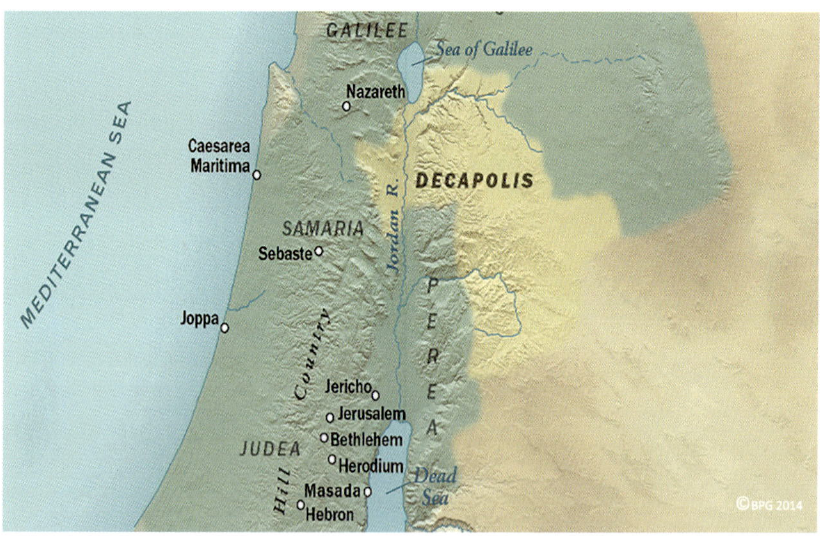

Figure 5.7, Jesus' Public Mission

Jesus performed his first miracle at Cana, close to the city of Nazareth.

On the hill behind Nazareth is Sepphoris, the capital city under Herod Antipas, a city with a mixed population of Jews and Romans.

Jesus lived and worked very close to the international highway where people were coming and going, speaking other languages, and holding various religious worldviews and observances of Jewish law. Jesus then moved his ministry to Capernaum.

Figure 5.8, Cities Along the International Highway

The international highway comes up the Mediterranean coast from Egypt, then moves through Capernaum on the Sea of Galilee, and then northeast to Damascus. Thus, Capernaum was a strategic location for Jesus' Galilean ministry.

Figure 5.10 illustrates how the international highway passes

Figure 5.9, The International Highway

Figure 5.10, The Arbel Pass

through the Arbel pass to Capernaum, which is on the northern coast of the Sea of Galilee.

On the far side of the Sea of Galilee is Gentile territory, where the story of the demon-possessed man took place.

Capernaum was a fishing town and the home of Peter and other disciples of Jesus.

Jesus spent a lot of time in a synagogue, like the white synagogue in Capernaum, which was most likely built centuries later on the site of

Figure 5.11, Capernaum

the original synagogue. The octagon-shaped church closer to the Sea of Galilee is built over the traditional site of the home of Peter.

Figure 5.12, Traditional Site of the Mount of Beatitudes

In his kingdom ministry, Jesus began to preach, teach, heal and cast out demons. In Matthew chapter 5, Jesus gives one of his early sermons about the Beatitudes on the Sermon on the Mount. Figure 5.12 shows a natural amphitheater on the coastline of the Sea of Galilee just west of Capernaum, in which Jesus could have been speaking along the water's edge down below, being heard all the way up the hill.

Jesus is a new Moses delivering God's new Torah, requiring people to have a righteousness that exceeds that of the Pharisees and the Scribes of his day.

Jesus' Phoenician ministry included the two cities of Tyre and Sidon, shown in Figure 5.13.

Figure 5.13, Phoenician Territory

Although Jesus was sent primarily to the lost sheep of Israel, he reached out to people who were outside the fold. Like Elisha, Jesus ministered to a Syrophoenician "Canaanite" woman.

JESUS' KINGDOM MISSION

Jesus' kingdom mission started with the announcement of the arrival of the kingdom, the central theme of his ministry. Jesus brought about the beginning of a new era in which believers would actively take part in the new kingdom.

THE KINGDOM REVEALED

In his mission, we see Jesus revealing his kingdom through his mighty deeds. The blind see; the lame walk; the deaf hear; the sick are healed; the dead are raised; the poor and the lost are received; sinners are forgiven; the cursed creation is restored; demons are cast out; and lives are changed (Luke 7:21–22). The people witness the signs of God's kingdom.[24]

"We modern people think of miracles as the suspension of the natural order, but Jesus meant them to be the restoration of the natural order. The Bible tells us that God did not originally make the world to have disease, hunger, and death in it. Jesus has come to redeem where it is wrong and heal the world where it is broken. His miracles are not just proofs that he has power but also wonderful foretastes of what he is going to do with that power. Jesus' miracles are not just a challenge to our minds, but a promise to our hearts, that the world we all want is coming."

–Timothy J. Keller[25]

---

24 Bartholomew and Goheen, 137–138.

25 "The Reason for God: Belief in an Age of Skepticism," GoodReads, accessed October 5, 2023, https://www.goodreads.com/quotes/386973-we-modern-people-think-of-miracles-as-the-suspension-of.

JEWISH VS. CHRISTIAN ESCHATOLOGY

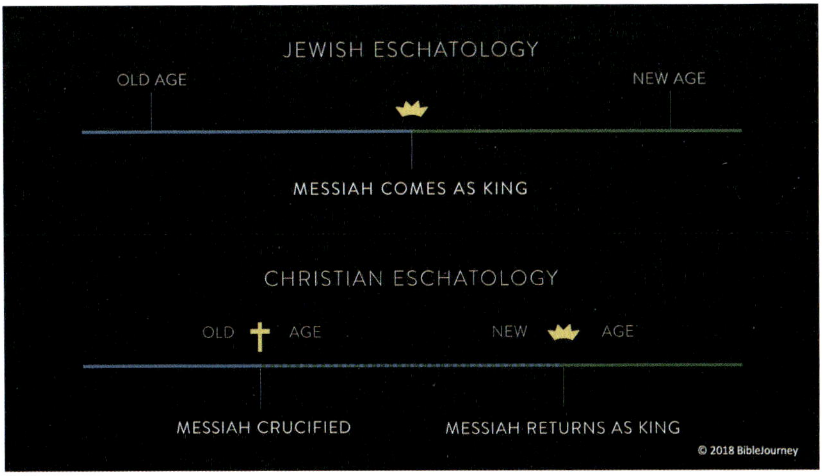

Figure 5.14, Jewish vs. Christian Echatology

As shown in Figure 5.14, in Jewish thought, the Messiah would bring about the end of the Old Age and usher in the New Age at one moment in history. What Jesus introduced was a surprise: an overlap of the old age and the age to come.

The evidence of the coming age was seen in power over sin and disease and the gifting of the Holy Spirit. Those are samples or deposits of the coming kingdom.

Jews believed in a sharp break between the Old Age and the New Age. Jesus introduced an unexpected nuance of a period of overlap. This is sometimes called "inaugurated eschatology" because the realities of the New Age are present but not fully realized.

Jesus ministered to people who represent classes without privilege. Jesus spent a lot of time with women, who were not eligible to be witnesses in court. They were his patrons and disciples. A shepherd was considered a profession without honor. Filled with compassion, Jesus healed the sick, the disabled and the demonized. He touched some people to scandalize others who thought that it was more important to be ritually pure than to care for others. Jesus' ministry cuts across every category, and every single person, whether young or old, male or female, well or sick. Every single person is eligible for God's mercy. Every single person was eligible to be a missionary, including women, lepers, shepherds, Samaritans and Gentiles, who he saw as sheep without a shepherd and who were considered ineligible in their culture.

Jesus demonstrated the power of prayer, often withdrawing to pray to his Father for strength, and even finding a way to be alone with the Father to pray all night.

Jesus brought radical new teaching, which consisted of

- Love of one's enemies
- Unconditional forgiveness
- Readiness to suffer for the kingdom

Jesus' teaching challenged the status quo, particularly aspects of the oral tradition of the Pharisees, which led to significant opposition (John 15:18–20).

Jesus demanded a decision. His followers are told that the decision is resolute and urgent (Luke 9:57–62), radical (Luke 9:23 ff.; 13:24), costly (Luke 14:25–33; Matthew 19:16–24) and eternal (Luke 16:26). Believers will enter the realm of the kingdom and be blessed with forgiveness and a renewed life. However, these gifts come with responsibility for righteousness, justice and love.

Jesus had authority over *everything*—disease, sin, nature, disability and even death—comprehensive authority. Jesus reversed the curse which the Devil introduced into the world in the Garden of Eden—the curse of sin, shame, suffering, and the Serpent. Jesus brought honor where there was shame, healing where there was disease, wholeness where there was brokenness. Jesus freed people from captivity to the Devil. Jesus sought to fix the biggest problem of humanity—what's in our hearts—which is going to determine our eternal destiny. As Jesus sent out his disciples, he gave them power to raise people from the dead, which is still going around the world.

Jesus used his authority not only to express his compassion but also to demonstrate that he was the Son of God. Although Jesus did not heal everyone, he gave people adequate evidence that they can trust his authority and trust his heart. He let people know that he was the same God who led Israel in the desert and who did all the miracles of provision and healing. Jesus gave bread in the desert in the Old Testament. He wanted people to recognize him as the God who had been with them before.

THE PASSION

The Passion Week is the climax of each of the Gospels. The Passion week started with Jesus entering Jerusalem on a donkey, fulfilling the prophecy of Zechariah 9:9.

As shown in Figure 5.15, Jesus entered Jerusalem from Bethpage.

He crossed over the Mount of Olives, mounted a donkey, rode through the Kidron Valley, and entered the Temple.

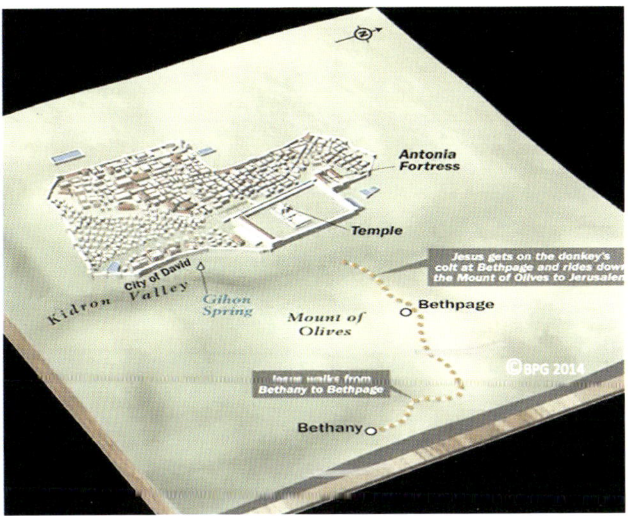

Figure 5.15, Jesus' Passion Week Entrance to Jerusalem

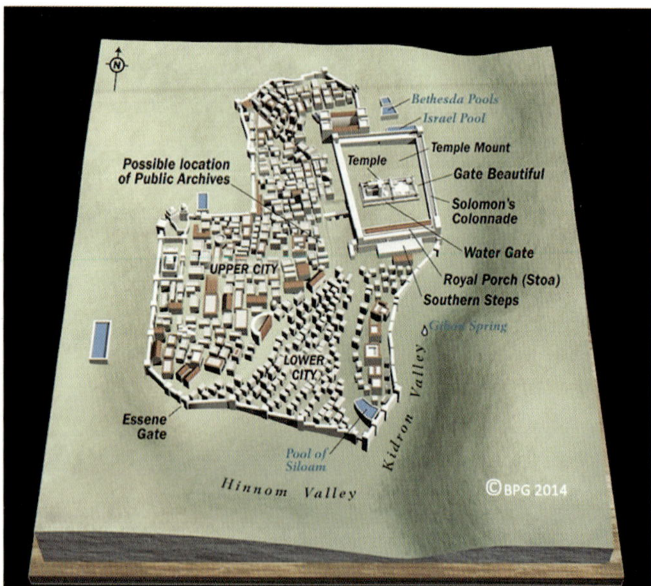

Figure 5.16, The Old City of Jerusalem

Figure 5.16 shows a closer view of the Old City of Jerusalem looking north.

The Temple Mount and the Temple are in the upper right corner. The City of David and the location of David's palace are just inside the city wall in the lower right, extending from the southern steps of the Temple Mount down to the Pool of Siloam, the lowest point and the location of Jesus' healing of a blind man.

The Kidron Valley is to the east of the city, and the Hinnom Valley is to the south.

The Gihon Spring is just outside the city walls on the eastern side. Hezekiah, the king who reigned during the time when Assyria was consolidating its control over its empire, strengthened the defense of Jerusalem, including the digging of a tunnel which routed water from the Gihon Spring to the pool of Siloam inside the city wall, securing a water supply for the city of Jerusalem (2 Kings 20:20; 2 Chronicles 32:30).

HEROD ANTIPAS' PALACE

Figure 5.17, Herod Antipas' Palace

Herod Antipas' palace, shown along the bottom of Figure 5.17, was the location of Jesus' trial. The Temple Mount is in the top left corner.

Figure 5.18 is a picture of modern-day Jerusalem taken from the Mount of Olives, which overlooks the Temple Mount.

In the foreground are sarcophagi, or bone boxes. Jesus came over this hill, the Mount of Olives, rode across the Kidron Valley, and entered the Temple during Passion Week, on his way to suffering and

Figure 5.18, Modern View of Jerusalem

death on a cross. Jesus then cleansed the Temple because the house of prayer had been turned into a den of thieves.

In his three years of ministry, Jesus dodged Jerusalem, and whenever people tried to trap him in a question, he outwitted them. However, during the Passion Week, Jesus walked in, and surprisingly gave them every opportunity to do what they wanted. He even confessed to blasphemy, and when he was given a chance to answer for himself, he didn't answer. At that point, it became clear that he had chosen *this* time. He had the authority to avoid execution, but he gave up his life as a martyr.

DEATH, RESURRECTION AND ASCENSION

Jesus underwent three trials, and he was brutally beaten, flogged and scourged on our behalf. But that, as we know, is not the end of the story. Everything the Jewish leaders, the Roman authorities and the Devil himself threw at Jesus was overturned at the resurrection. Jesus' death, resurrection and ascension completed his mission of atonement on our behalf.

Although Jesus had said all along, you should know from the Scriptures that the Son of Man must suffer and die, no one had been expecting him to be one of the Temple sacrificial lambs. When Jesus died on the cross, he was outside the city gates in a dump, completely impure. He had been stripped and shamed in public, and yet a Roman soldier said, "Surely he was the Son of God!" (Matthew 27:54).

Following his death, Jesus appeared to over 500 people (1 Corinthians 15:6). Then, in the Great Commission, he commissioned his disciples to take the Gospel to the ends of the Earth (Matthew 28:19-20). Jesus now reigns at the right hand of God.

WHO IS JESUS?

Jesus is the good news. He is the Gospel, and he has made a way for us to be restored to the garden relationship, as if we had never sinned. John tells us that Jesus is the eternal Son of God (John 1:1–15). The writer of Hebrews notes that "the Son is the radiance of God's glory and the exact representation of his being" (1:3). Jesus is the Creator and Sustainer of the world (Hebrews 1:1–3; John 1:1). Jesus is superior to all Old Testament figures and institutions, such as the prophets, angels, Moses, Aaron, the Levitical priesthood and Melchizedek (Hebrews 1–10).

JESUS' FULFILLMENT OF THE OLD TESTAMENT

Following his resurrection, in his appearance to his disciples, Luke tells us, "beginning with Moses and all the Prophets, [Jesus] explained to them what was said in all the Scriptures concerning himself" (Luke 24:27).

The whole Old Testament pointed to Jesus, most obviously through predictive prophecies, such as the first messianic prediction of Genesis 3:15, the virgin birth predicted in Isaiah 7:14, the return from Egypt predicted by Hosea 11:1, and numerous references to the final Day of the Lord.

Another breathtaking way "all the Scriptures" pointed to Christ was through "types." A type is a person, event or place which contained a future-facing dimension not necessarily recognized by the initial audience. A list of types that the New Testament unpacks would include Adam, Abraham, Israel, Moses, Joshua, Elijah, Elisha, David, Solomon, Passover, the Exodus, the Old Covenant, Pentecost, the Sabbath, the Tabernacle and the Temple, Melchizedek, the Levitical priesthood, sacrificial lambs, purification vessels, shepherds, bread, water, servants, the Word, rabbis, light, and land. For this chapter, we will simply touch on the following few examples:

- Whereas Israel clearly failed in its mission to be a light to the nations, Jesus successfully completed the mission given to Israel. Pentecost launched a new period in which Jesus gathered his followers as the new Israel to continue the mission to the nations.
- Whereas the Sabbath was a periodic means of rest, Jesus is the ultimate Sabbath rest for believers.

- The Levitical priesthood was temporary and not totally effective in offering sacrifices for the sins of man. Jesus, however, not only became the perfect High Priest from the line of Melchizedek, but also the perfect, once-and-for-all sacrifice for the sins of man.

Jesus is the heart of the story. Jesus is The Story.

For a more complete discussion of the ways in which Jesus fulfills the Old Testament, refer to Appendix B.

ACT 4 KEY TAKEAWAYS

- The Word became flesh (incarnation) and tabernacled among us again (John 1:14).
- Jesus selected the 12 apostles, representing the 12 tribes of Israel, to continue the mission.
- Through his death, resurrection and ascension, Jesus redeemed the world, and he reigns at the right hand of God.
- Jesus succeeded where Israel failed.
- The kingdom arrived but is not fully complete—the "already but not yet."
- Jesus is the heart of the story; he is The Story.

ACT 4 CHALLENGE QUESTION

Have you accepted Jesus as Lord, not just Savior?

ADDITIONAL REFLECTION QUESTIONS

- What did you find surprising about this part of the Bible story?
- What else did you find interesting about this part of the Bible story?
- How has this part of the Bible story challenged your thinking?
- How has this part of the Bible story shaped your worldview?
- What will you do differently as a result of what you learned?
- Who will you tell about what you have learned?

Chapter 6

ACT 5 THE MISSION OF THE CHURCH: SPREADING THE NEWS OF THE KING

THE LENS WIDENS

In Genesis 1, we saw how the lens of the biblical camera started with a wide-angle view in the creation of the world. In Genesis 12, the lens of the camera narrowed from the entire world to the nation of Israel. As we explore the spreading of the good news, notice how once again the camera lens widens to the entire world, without losing the

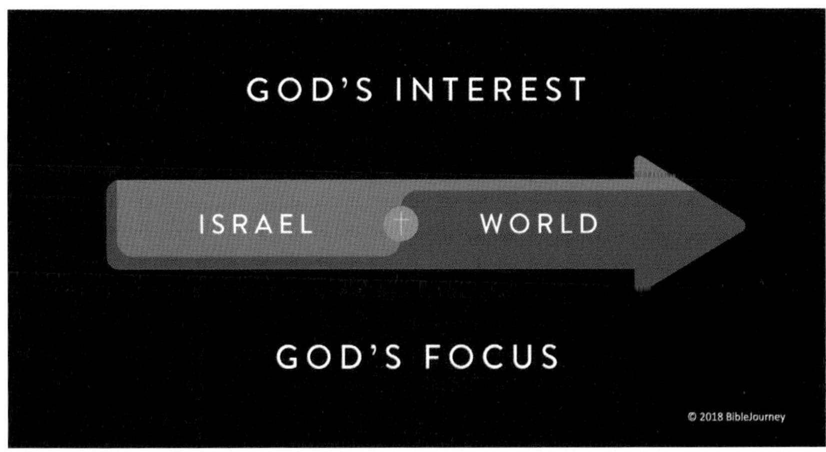

Figure 6.1, God's Interest and Focus

story of Israel, which has always been about anyone who is a member of the family of God.

The book of Acts gives us a glimpse into the continuing mission of Jesus, which is now the mission of the Church through his Spirit, and can be divided into two scenes:

- Scene One: From Jerusalem to Rome
- Scene Two: And into All the World

SCENE ONE: FROM JERUSALEM TO ROME

Pentecost in Acts fulfills an Old Testament promise of the outpouring of the Spirit (Isaiah 44:3; Joel 2:28–29; Zechariah 12:10). Recall Pentecost's agricultural significance as the Jewish feast of firstfruits of the wheat harvest and its historical significance of the giving of the Law at Mt. Sinai. At Pentecost in Acts, God's Spirit descends on the people, and they speak in tongues, empowered by the Spirit.

Pentcost: Babel Reversed

Confused & speaking in many languages	Understanding & hearing in many languages
Scattered	United
Humanity reaching towards heaven	God reaching towards humanity
People making a name for themselves	People waiting on God to send the Spirit

© 2018 BibleJourney

Figure 6.2, Pentecost: Babel Reversed

At Pentecost in Acts, we witness how Babel (Genesis 11) is reversed.

At Babel, language is confused from one to many, whereas at Pentecost, the people of various tongues understand one another. At Babel, the people are scattered, whereas at Pentecost the people are united. At Babel, the people reach toward heaven, whereas at Pentecost, God reaches toward humanity. At Babel, the people try to make a name for themselves, whereas at Pentecost, the people wait on God to send the Spirit's power.

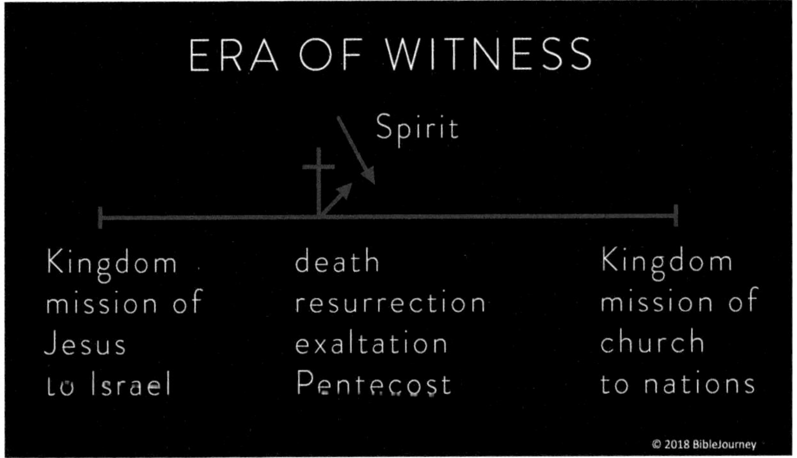

Figure 6.3, Era of Witness

The provision of the Spirit at Pentecost allows for the start of the mission of the Church to the nations.

Israel clearly failed in its mission to be a light to the nations. However, Jesus successfully completed the mission given to Israel. Pentecost launched a new period in which Jesus gathered the new Israel (i.e., followers of Christ) to continue the mission to the nations, a mission that continues through the Church today.

Jesus conveyed to the disciples the mission of the Church in Acts 1:8. "But you will receive power when the Holy Spirit comes on you; and you will be my witnesses in Jerusalem, and in all Judea and Samaria, and to the ends of the earth."

"Acts narrates the progress of the Gospel from a small gathering of Jewish disciples of the earthly Jesus in Jerusalem, across formidable cultic, ethnic, relational, and geographical boundaries, to Paul's bold and unhindered preaching of the risen and ascended Jesus to Gentiles in Rome. Acts is unmistakably a story of missionary expansion, which is announced in 1:8 and confirmed along the way with the so-called progress reports."

–Brian Rosner[26]

Throughout the book of Acts, we see the progress of the Church in moving the Gospel from Jerusalem to Samaria and Judea and to the ends of the Earth.

"The ending of Acts is truly an opening to the continuing life of the messianic people, as it continues to preach the kingdom and teach the things concerning Jesus both boldly and without hindrance."

–Luke Timothy Johnson[27]

THE GOSPEL SPREADS

The apostle Paul is often considered the greatest missionary. As the apostle to the Gentiles, Paul carried the Gospel throughout the Greco-Roman Empire.

On his first missionary journey, Paul concentrated on Asia Minor, or modern-day Turkey.

God's plan was to move this *Jewish* movement into Gentile territory, something that was very hard for many to accept.

---

26 Brian S. Rosner, "The Progress of the Word," in Witness to the Gospel: The Theology of Acts, ed. I. Howard Marshall and David Peterson (Grand Rapids: Eerdmans, 1998), 221. https://www.thegospelcoalition.org/themelios/article/the-characterization-of-peter-and-the-message-of-acts/

27 Luke Timothy Johnson, *The Acts of the Apostles* (Collegeville, MN: Liturgical Press, 2006), 474–476.

Figure 6.4, Paul's 1st Missionary Journey

Figure 6.5, Paul's 2nd Missionary Journey

Figure 6.6, Paul's 3rd Missionary Journey

Paul's second missionary journey was the journey that moved the Gospel from Asia to Europe (Greece).

The third missionary journey is a return to places from the earlier journeys and looks much like Paul's second journey.

Figure 6.7, Jewish Diaspora

Many Jews were living in Diaspora, or dispersion. The black dots of Figure 6.7 show places where Jews had a concentrated population.

Paul used this dispersion to his advantage. Recall that Paul goes to the Jews first, then to the Gentiles. The early *Christian* movement was a Jewish movement. While the early churches often suffered at the hands of local Jewish communities, it was in the *synagogues* that both Jews and Gentiles first heard the Gospel as a *Jewish* message. Acts 28:23b tells us, "He witnessed to them from morning till evening, explaining about the kingdom of God, and from the Law of Moses and from the Prophets he tried to persuade them about Jesus."

ROMAN ROADS

While the Romans were known for their severe persecution of Christians, it was actually the Romans who in several ways facilitated the spread of the Gospel.

Figure 6.8, Ancient Roman Road

Along with establishing the peace and security of the Pax Romana, the Romans built roads like this part of the Ignatian Way in Macedonia that made it possible for the Gospel to spread. These roads connected the major cities of the whole Roman Empire from Europe to Asia.

SCENE TWO: AND INTO ALL THE WORLD (OUR PLACE IN THE STORY)

The story of Acts continues today, and we are in it. We are *commanded* to continue the mission. Just like Israel, we are tasked with being channels of blessings (Genesis 12:2–3; Galatians 3:14), model people (Exodus 19:3–6; 1 Peter 2:9) and a light to the world (Isaiah

49:6; Matthew 5:14–16).[28] Living out Jesus brings social and cultural transformation.

We continue Jesus' mission of making the kingdom known, and the mission of the Early Church in bearing faithful witness. We are called to be God's partner in rescuing humanity and restoring all of creation from the effects of sin. Therefore, we must attach ourselves to the Lord through prayer, confession, listening to his Word, and being in community.

"Put your nose into the Bible every day.
It is your spiritual food. And then share it.
Make a vow not to be a lukewarm Christian."
–KIRK CAMERON[29]

"We are the Bibles the world is reading; we are the creeds the world is needing; we are the sermons the world is heeding."
–BILLY GRAHAM[30]

---

28 Bartholomew and Goheen, 198.

29 "7 Provocative Kirk Cameron Quotes About the Christian Lifestyle," Motivated2Inspire, accessed October 5, 2023, https://motivated2inspire.com/35-kirk-cameron-quotes-to-inspire-passion-for-the-kingdom-of-god/.

30 "Billy Graham > Quotes > Quotable Quote," Goodreads.com, accessed October 5, 2023, https://www.goodreads.com/quotes/306084-we-are-the-bibles-the-world-is-reading-we-are.

ACT 5 KEY TAKEAWAYS

- The Spirit descends upon the Church at Pentecost as predicted (Acts 2:21; Joel 2:28–32).
- The mission to spread the Gospel (the "good news") to the ends of the Earth continues through the Church (Matthew 28:19).
- We are story dwellers, not just story tellers, uniquely equipped for our God-given purpose.

ACT 5 CHALLENGE QUESTION

How has God uniquely equipped you for your role in Act 5, what parts of your story do you see reflecting kingdom living, and how is the Holy Spirit nudging you regarding use of your spiritual gifts in the calling that God has planned for you?

ADDITIONAL REFLECTION QUESTIONS

- What did you find surprising about this part of the Bible story?
- What else did you find interesting about this part of the Bible story?
- How has this part of the Bible story challenged your thinking?
- How has this part of the Bible story shaped your worldview?
- What will you do differently as a result of what you learned?
- Who will you tell about what you have learned?

Chapter 7

ACT 6 REDEMPTION COMPLETED: THE RETURN OF THE KING

In Act 6, the return of the King, redemption is fully completed in the book of Revelation. The story ends with a new heaven and a new earth in which everything is restored, and we are once again face-to-face in the presence of the awesome Almighty.

PROPHECY AND APOCALYPTIC LITERATURE

While many books of the Bible clearly belong to one literary genre or another, Revelation has characteristics of *multiple* genres and defies

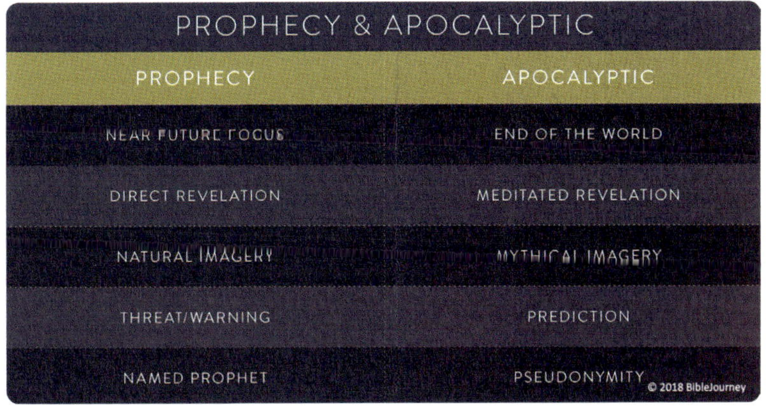

PROPHECY & APOCALYPTIC

PROPHECY	APOCALYPTIC
NEAR FUTURE FOCUS	END OF THE WORLD
DIRECT REVELATION	MEDITATED REVELATION
NATURAL IMAGERY	MYTHICAL IMAGERY
THREAT/WARNING	PREDICTION
NAMED PROPHET	PSEUDONYMITY

© 2018 BibleJourney

Figure 7.1, Prophecy and Apocalyptic Literature

easy classification. Revelation is a letter, but it is also a book of prophecy and an apocalyptic text. Prophecy and apocalyptic text differ in a number of ways.

One of the biggest differences is that apocalyptic literature uses mythical imagery, or symbols. The following chart shows some of the symbology that John *defines* in the book of Revelation.

SYMBOLS JOHN HIMSELF USES

SYMBOL	REPRESENTS
THE GOLDEN LAMPSTANDS (1:20)	CHURCHES
THE SEVEN STARS (1:20)	ANGELS
THE GREAT DRAGON (12:9)	SATAN
THE SEVEN HEADS (17:9-10)	SEVEN MOUNTAINS SEVEN KINGS
THE HARLOT (17:18)	THE GREAT CITY = ROME

© 2018 BibleJourney

Figure 7.2, Symbols John Himself Uses

While much has been made of the meaning of these symbols and the way the world will come to an end, we are going to keep our discussion at the overall story level.

There are a number of things the book of Revelation gives us a window into. In Revelation 21, we get a glimpse of the ultimate hope of a Christian follower—the Gospel is a message of restoration. The old order passes away. We get a new city, a new garden, with representatives from every nation and every language.

Sin and its effects are removed. The world will finally be healed of all the brokenness that has existed from the time of Adam and Eve's rebellion—not just people, but *all* of creation. We will have come full circle from Garden to Garden, and we will live in the direct presence of God.

"Very often people have come to the New Testament with the presumption that 'going to heaven when you die' is the implicit point of it all... They acquire that viewpoint from somewhere, but not from the New Testament."

–N. T. Wright[31]

BIBLICAL BOOKENDS: RESTORATION OF ALL THAT WAS LOST

There are several ways that the New Testament will bring to a climax what was disrupted at the beginning of the Old Testament. The following table shows a comparison of the opening chapters of Genesis and closing chapters of Revelation—the Bible's bookends—to illustrate how God will restore all that was lost.

BIBLICAL BOOKENDS

GENESIS	REVELATION
CREATION OF HEAVEN AND EARTH (GEN 1:1–2:4)	CREATION OF NEW HEAVEN AND EARTH (REV 21:1-5)
EDEN SANCTUARY, RIVER AND TREE OF LIFE (GEN 2:4-17)	NEW JERUSALEM SANCTUARY, RIVER AND TREE OF LIFE (REV 21:9–22:2)
"MARRIAGE" OF ADAM AND EVE (GEN 2:18-25)	MARRIAGE OF CHRIST AND THE CHURCH (REV 19:5-9; 21:1-9)
SATAN AND THE WOMAN (GEN 3:1-13)	SATAN AND THE WOMAN (REV 12:1-17)
DEATH ENTERS CREATION (GEN 3:14-19)	DEATH DESTROYED (REV 20:14-15)
BABYLON BUILT; JUDGMENT ON NATIONS (GEN 10:10; 11:1-4)	BABYLON DESTROYED; JUDGMENT ON NATIONS (REV 14:6–20)
REDEEMER PROMISED (GEN 3:15)	REDEEMER REIGNS (REV 20:1-6; 21:22-27; 22:3-5)

© 2018 BibleJourney

Figure 7.3, Bibical Bookends

Both Genesis and Revelation create a new heaven and a new earth. The Garden sanctuaries mirror one another with a river and a tree of life. The heavenly moment with Adam and Eve prior to sin

31 N. T. Wright, "New Heavens, New Earth," in *Called to One Hope* (ed. John Colwell; Carlisle, UK: Paternoster, 2000), 33.

is paralleled by the marriage of Christ and the Church. Eve is the prototypical mother of all children, and Mary has to flee to Egypt to escape the killing of her child by Herod, much like we have the Devil in Revelation trying to kill the child of the woman. Death wasn't present in the Garden of Eden until the punishment of Adam and Eve, and in Revelation 20, death is destroyed. In Genesis 11 we experience the rebellion at Babel, and Babylon is destroyed in Revelation 14. Finally, the Redeemer is promised in Genesis 3:15, and the book of Revelation ends with the reign of the Redeemer who was promised—the seed of the woman.

There is a redemptive dimension in place for all the threats to God's creation and his purposes. Genesis 1–11 shows us the *beginning* of all things. When Revelation brings us to the end of all things, it is actually a *new beginning.*

"This is a God who acts in time and space on a linear arrow that goes from a beginning to a God-ordained end, and that end looks like the beginning."

–DR. TIMOTHY LANIAK[32]

32 Timothy S. Laniak, Bible Journey Program, accessed October 5, 2023, https://bible-journey.com.

ACT 6 KEY TAKEAWAYS

- Jesus will return to redeem and restore all of creation.
- Revelation contains apocalyptic literature with representative symbols.
- Jesus defeats the enemy in the supernatural, spiritual realm.
- Revelation 21 gives us a glimpse into the ultimate hope for us as a follower of Christ.
- The curses of the Fall are reversed, including death itself.
- We will once again be in a Garden, dwelling face-to-face with the Almighty God in peace and unity with fellow believers and all of God's creation.

ACT 6 CHALLENGE QUESTION

Armed with knowledge of the story, which loved ones or acquaintances do you need to reach out to and share the salvation message before it becomes too late?

I challenge you to take all of the challenge questions as well as your own questions for where you believe the Holy Spirit is nudging you to make changes in your life and act on them as you continue on your *own* journey.

ADDITIONAL REFLECTION QUESTIONS

- What did you find surprising about this part of the Bible story?
- What else did you find interesting about this part of the Bible story?
- How has this part of the Bible story challenged your thinking?
- How has this part of the Bible story shaped your worldview?
- What will you do differently as a result of what you learned?
- Who will you tell about what you have learned?

Chapter 8

RECAPPING THE STORY

The story began with the amazing opening scene of creation, in which God established his kingdom and gave his image-bearers their unique role.

The Fall is a story of rebellion in the kingdom. The Fall told us the story of two individuals who sought to become autonomous, and as a result radically altered the course of human history.

In Act 3, the process of redemption was initiated, starting with the selection of Abraham, which led to the nation of Israel. "The Old Testament portrays God's patience with his rebellious covenant people and his promises to rescue sinners and restore his broken world."[33]

"The Intertestamental Period bridged the testaments through the preparation for the Gospel."[34]

In the Gospels, redemption was accomplished with the coming of the King. The Gospels announce "that God has fulfilled his ancient promises and demonstrated his goodness and loving kindness by sending Jesus Christ, our Savior."[35]

---

33 Brian J. Tabb, *1–2 Timothy and Titus, A 12-Week Study* (Wheaton: Crossway, 2017), 8.

34 Cooley, n.p.

35 Tabb, 8.

Act 5 shows us the mission of the Church, which is to spread the good news of the King. "Acts records how Jesus' followers continued his mission by proclaiming the Gospel in the power of the Holy Spirit among all nations."[36]

The story will end with the completion of redemption when the King returns. We will receive a new heaven and a new earth in which everything is restored, and we will be once again face-to-face in the presence of the awesome Almighty.

ASSURED ENDING

You may have noticed that many movies contain a familiar storyline. They often start out with a guy and a girl, trouble ensues, a new guy comes on the scene, a new relationship blossoms, and finally we see "happily ever after." Well, that may be an oversimplification, but the point is that you have a fairly good sense of where the story is going without having to watch the full story, and you know the story will have a good ending.

> ***"I've read the last page of the Bible;***
> ***it's all going to turn out alright."***
> –Billy Graham[37]

The framework you see here is the framework of God's story. Once you know the story, you can place each of the characters and other details within the story, and you can have hope for a good ending regardless of what happens during the story. One major difference, however, is that you are a story *dweller* within God's story, not simply a story *teller* or story *observer*.

36 Ibid.

37 "I've Read the Last Page of the Bible," SermonQuotes.com, accessed October 6, 2023, https://sermonquotes.com/billy-graham-2/11206-ive-read-last-page-bible-billy-graham.html.

Chapter 9

CLOSING PERSPECTIVES

We just covered about 2,000 years of history, or we could say, "His story."

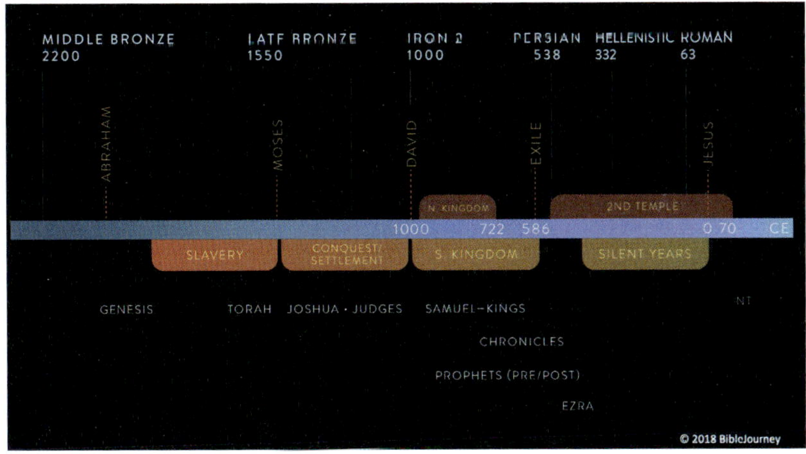

Figure 9.1, Timeline of the Bible

HIS STORY–OUR STORY

We saw creation unfold and the Fall of mankind at a time unknown to us. We saw God begin the process of redemption approximately 4,000 years ago, and we watched the hero of the story come on the scene 2,000 years ago.

Act 5 of the story continues today as we do our part in responding to the Great Commission while we await the second coming of our King.

"Until I come, devote yourself to the public reading of Scripture, to preaching and to teaching."
–1 TIMOTHY 4:13

STORY DWELLERS, NOT JUST STORY TELLERS

In Act 5, we saw how we are story dwellers, not just story tellers. Though we are not the hero, we have an important part to play in the story.[38] As story dwellers, we are uniquely prepared and called to partner with God in redeeming his creation. Following our calling in life means "to become who God created you to be and do what he created you to do."[39]

YOUR GIFTING AND CALLING

Whereas a calling is "God's fulfillment of who you are in a specific role in relationship with Him to accomplish His purposes,"[40] a spiritual gift is "an ability that is given and empowered by the Holy Spirit for God's purposes, such as teaching, encouraging or prophesying."[41]

According to R. J. Scherba, God's calling has three parts:

1. God's universal call to all people for salvation:
"For God so loved the world that he gave his one and only Son, that whoever believes in him shall not perish but have eternal life." (John 3:16)

38 Thornton, 52–54.

39 R. J. Scherba, "Questions and Answers About Christian Calling," November 5, 2023, https://rjchristiancoaching.com/questions-and-answers-about-christian-calling/?doing_wp_cron=1699210929.5855429172515869140625.

40 Ibid.

41 Ibid.

Your calling begins when you ask Jesus to forgive you of your sins, and you give control of your life to Him.

2. God's general call to all Christians to love Him and love other people:

[Jesus] answered, "Love the Lord your God with all your heart and with all your soul and with all your strength and with all your mind; and love your neighbor as yourself." (Luke 10:27)

We answer God's general call as we grow in basic discipleship, learning how to pray, read the Bible, live and serve in Christian community, become like Him, and reach others for Christ.

3. God's specific call to each Christian to make a difference for Him in a unique way:

It is in Christ that we find out who we are and what we are living for. (Ephesians 1:11)

This Bible verse shows that calling is first about who you are, and second about what you do! As you become genuinely yourself in relationship with Him and people, you will more fully do your calling.[42]

Jordan Raymor suggests three questions to ask yourself when discerning God's calling on your life:

1. *What am I passionate about?* Said more meaningfully, what are the things that you care deeply about that build God's kingdom and fit into this incredible metanarrative of God's overall plan for his people whom he loves and with whom he wants a relationship?
2. *What gifts has God given me?* Consider examining your resume, listing your skills and qualifications, and asking others for their input. Consider also the most significant accomplishments in

42 Ibid.

all aspects of your life, and highlight the ones that gave you the most satisfaction and joy.

3. *Where do I have the greatest opportunity to love others?* Consider not only your existing relationships, but also all those with whom you come in contact with each day.

Jordan notes that these questions will assist you in discerning where God has called you to put your energy on his behalf.[43]

In addition to answering Jordan's questions, I suggest the following:

1. Write down the most significant moments in your life, whether they are happy memories or low points.
2. Ask God why he has given you these skills, qualifications, accomplishments, joys and crucibles.
3. Challenge yourself by asking how each of these aspects has prepared you for your calling.
4. Seek others who can help you in this calling, either by directly assisting you, or indirectly supporting you through means such as mentoring and prayer.
5. Act on your kingdom calling, and watch how God sustains you at every step.

FINAL EXERCISE

Now that you have finished reading, take some time to again write down some high-level facts about the Bible. These can be statements about the Bible that you believe are true, or they can be simple facts such as the number of books, or the number of authors. When you are finished, go back to the exercise you previously set aside and compare your notes from each exercise.

---

43 Jordan Raynor, "Work and Rest: 3 Questions for Discerning Your Calling," https://www.cru.org/us/en/train-and-grow/life-and-relationships/work-and-rest/3-questions-for-discerning-your-calling.html.

If you would like to go deeper into understanding God's Word and how it applies to your life, visit https://biblejourney.com.

"Apply yourself wholly to the Scriptures,
and apply the Scriptures wholly to yourself."
–JOHANN A. BENGEL[44]

CLOSING

I hope that this journey through the Bible has not only helped you become better acquainted with the Story of God and his covenant people, but that it has challenged you to discover your own individual story within the larger story, and more importantly, to act on your calling.

"Don't fall into the trap of studying the Bible
without doing what it says."
–FRANCIS CHAN[45]

May God bless you in your journey.

44 James Callen, "Christian Quotes About the Bible," Toliveischrist.com, accessed October 5, 2023, http://toliveischrist.com/quotes-about-the-bible/.

45 Francis Chan Quotes, QuoteFancy, accessed October 5, 2023, https://quotefancy.com/quote/805701/Francis-Chan-Don-t-fall-into-the-trap-of-studying-the-Bible-without-doing-what-it-says, accessed November 5, 2023.

Appendix A

INTERTESTAMENTAL PERIOD: GOING DEEPER

Our focus on the Intertestamental Period will be on the significance of the period in preparation for the Gospel. However, before we move into this aspect, the following key dates and events are provided for reference.

HISTORICAL OVERVIEW

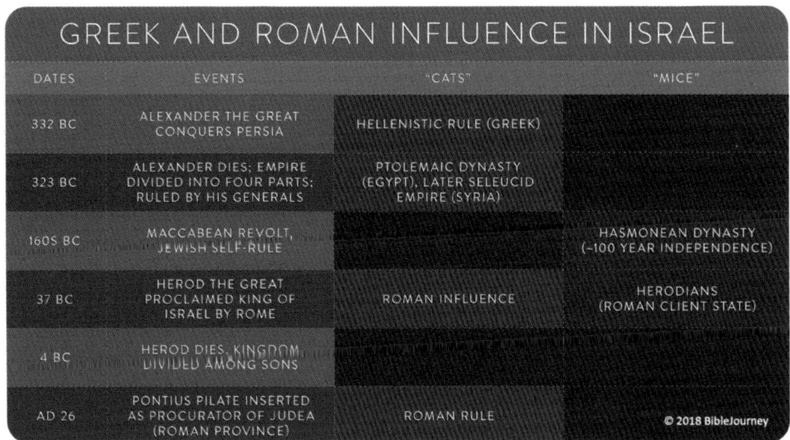

GREEK AND ROMAN INFLUENCE IN ISRAEL

DATES	EVENTS	"CATS"	"MICE"
332 BC	ALEXANDER THE GREAT CONQUERS PERSIA	HELLENISTIC RULE (GREEK)	
323 BC	ALEXANDER DIES; EMPIRE DIVIDED INTO FOUR PARTS; RULED BY HIS GENERALS	PTOLEMAIC DYNASTY (EGYPT), LATER SELEUCID EMPIRE (SYRIA)	
160S BC	MACCABEAN REVOLT, JEWISH SELF-RULE		HASMONEAN DYNASTY (~100 YEAR INDEPENDENCE)
37 BC	HEROD THE GREAT PROCLAIMED KING OF ISRAEL BY ROME	ROMAN INFLUENCE	HERODIANS (ROMAN CLIENT STATE)
4 BC	HEROD DIES, KINGDOM DIVIDED AMONG SONS		
AD 26	PONTIUS PILATE INSERTED AS PROCURATOR OF JUDEA (ROMAN PROVINCE)	ROMAN RULE	

© 2018 BibleJourney

Figure A.1, Greek and Roman Influence in Israel

Recall that the Israelites were permitted to return to the Promised Land following the decree from Persian King Cyrus in 539 BC, fulfilling the promise of Deuteronomy 30:5–9. In 331 BC, Alexander the Great conquered the Persians, so Israel was under Greek rule. In 323 BC, Alexander died and left no heir, so a struggle ensued among his generals.

From 311 to 198 BC, Egypt again cast its shadow over Israel with the rule of the Ptolemites. From 198 to 164 BC, Israel was ruled by the Seleucids of Syria.

In 167 BC, Antiochus IV desecrated the Temple by setting up an altar within it to Zeus, the preeminent god of the Greek pantheon, and sacrificing a pig, the most unclean animal in Jewish Law (1 Maccabees 1:21–23). In 164 BC, Judah Maccabee cleansed the Temple, a deliverance event memorialized in the Feast of Hanukkah (1 Maccabees 4:41–61).

Like the Exodus, the Maccabean Revolt was a defining moment in Jewish history. God had delivered his people, restored his Temple, and vindicated his Law. Since God had visited his people in this dramatic act of redemption, there was an expectation that he would surely do so again as the Prophets had promised for so long. However, the Hasmonean kings that followed were deeply compromised by their affection for pagan, Hellenistic culture and a desire to maintain their political power.

In 142 BC, Seleucid rule was completely removed from Israel, and an 80-year period of Hasmonean self-rule followed.

Rome had been rising steadily since Seleucus I and Ptolemy I assumed rule over parts of the Greek Empire 200 years earlier, in 323 BC. In 63 BC, Pompeii the Great took Jerusalem, beginning a Roman presence which would last for approximately 500 years.

This is the history into which Jesus was born in 6 BC under the Judean rule of Herod the Great (37–4 BC).

THE THREAT CHANGES

Figure A.2 shows the extent of the Greek Empire in 300 BC. Here again a global superpower was ruling in both Europe and Asia and across the Middle East.

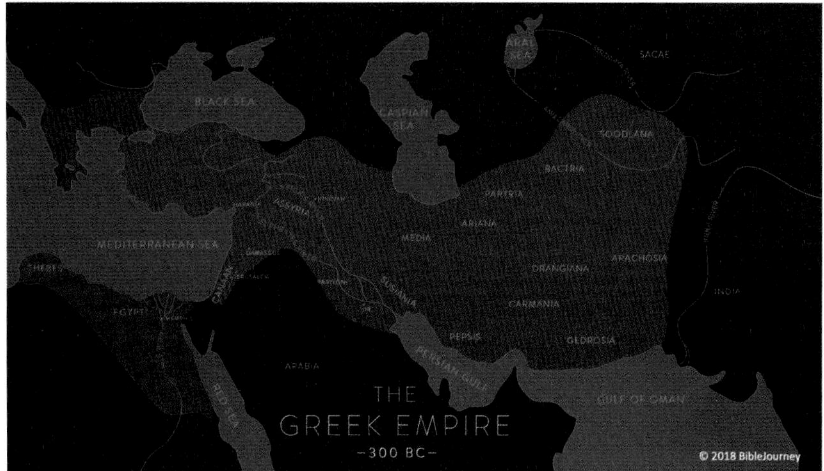

Figure A.2, The Greek Empire

As a result of Alexander the Great's conquest of the Persians in 331 BC, the threat to Israel changed to one of culture. The Greek Hellenistic culture saturated Israel's culture.

Torah scholars translated the Bible into Greek (the Septuagint). This began to undermine Israel's own cultural and religious integrity as the singular people of God, and pressure to conform to Hellenistic cultural patterns intensified.

THE ROMAN EMPIRE

Figure A.3 shows the extent of the Roman Empire in the first century.

Rome chose indirect rule—cooperative puppet kings and governors, consisting of the last of the Hasmoneans, Herod the Great and his descendants, and finally a series of Roman-appointed procurators,

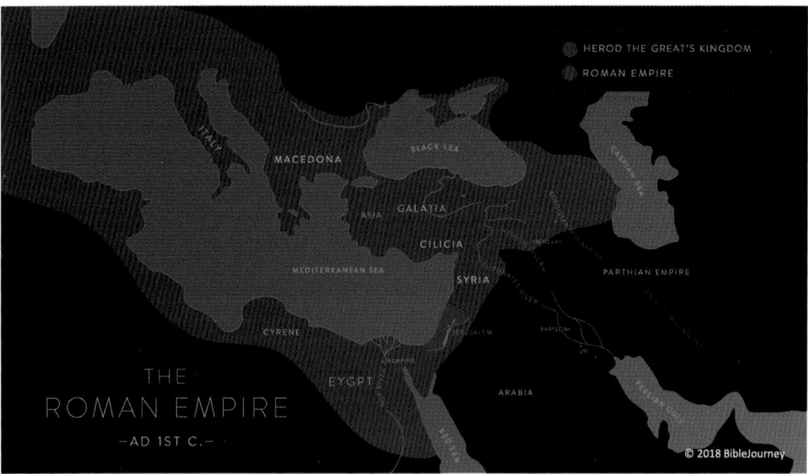

Figure A.3, The Roman Empire

or prefects, including Pontius Pilate. The Roman government also appointed the Temple's high priest. So frustration toward pagan rule now shifted to the powerful and brutal Rome, which utilized fear and intimidation, trampled on cultural sensitivities of their conquered peoples, taxed them into penury, forced their own brand of Hellenistic culture, and meted out savage punishment to all who opposed. The Jews identified Rome with Daniel's vision of the last and worst of the four "beasts" rising out of the sea (Daniel 7:7). Racial hatred of Gentiles increased, spilling over to Jews who collaborated with Rome. Local acts of rebellion were swiftly and violently put down, ending with mass crucifixions. During this time, 10 to 12 revolutionary movements arose around a messianic or quasi-messianic figure.

Rome had absorbed the Greek Empire, so the most extensive and powerful influence is called Greco-Roman.

THE "SILENT YEARS" (NOT REALLY)

The Intertestamental Period is sometimes referred to as the 400 Silent Years, because it is the period between the last Prophet of the Old Testament, Malachi, and when John the Baptist comes on the scene.

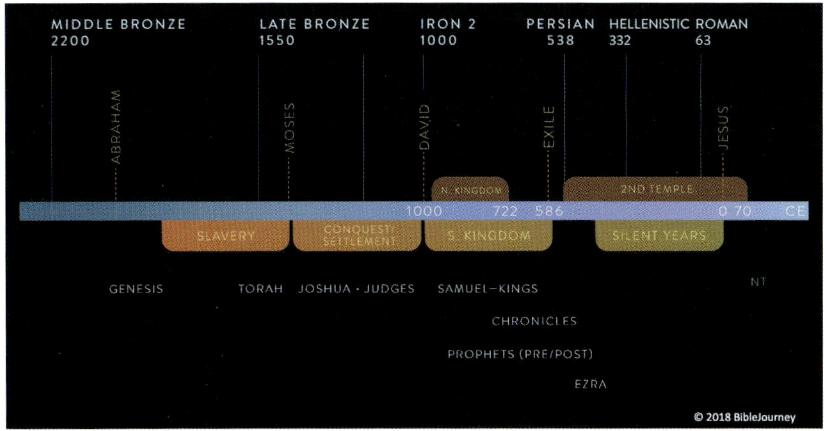

Figure A.4, Timeline of the Bible

Although we don't have prophetic literature during this time period, God was clearly working during this period in preparation for sending his Son into the world.

DIFFERING EXPRESSIONS OF ISRAEL'S HOPE

The 400-year Intertestamental Period between Malachi and Matthew was characterized by the following aspects:

- The Jews were scattered in the Diaspora as a result of God's instruments of judgment.
- Jews maintained their cultural distinctiveness, creating synagogues for Sabbath worship, prayer and study of the Scriptures.
- The Torah remained foundational.
- Synagogues provided educational, judicial, social, economic and political centers.

Israel's Faith continued to hold five fundamental beliefs:

- Monotheism: There is one God (Creator of the world and Ruler of history).
- Election: God had chosen Israel for a special purpose (Abrahamic covenant).

- Law (Torah): God had given Israel the Law to direct its way of life.
- Land and Temple: The land was holy because God dwelled with Israel.
- Hope for a Future Redemptive Act: God would complete his redemptive work.

Tensions were growing—oppression vs. hope, and pagan influence vs. faithfulness to the Torah.

Hatred intensified against Gentile oppressors and compromising Jews. Yet at the same time, hope grew for the coming kingdom of God. Israel readied itself for God's kingdom through hope, prayer, study and celebration. However, differing views emerged regarding how, when, and through whom the kingdom was to come, and how to live in the interim, summarized as follows:

- Pharisees created boundary markers (additional laws).
- Essenes withdrew (ritual purity and prayer).
- Sadducees strategically compromised and became the recognized representatives/teachers.
- Zealots violently revolted and became a subculture.
- Common people persisted with life's basics.

The **Pharisees** were Jewish nationalists. They became prominent in the synagogues as teachers of Law and oral tradition purportedly from Moses. They were inspired by an urgent sense of the need for revolutionary change: separate Israel completely from ideas and practices of pagans and teach radical obedience to the Torah. The Pharisees emphasized aspects of the Torah that marked uniqueness (circumcision, food laws, observing Sabbath), providing new significance as boundary markers from the faithless pagans. Many were ready to advance godly revolution with political activism and even violence. They were successful because they gave voice to some of the deepest desires of the people of Israel: longing for liberation, loyalty to the Torah, and a long-held hope for a renewed kingdom in which God himself would reign over his people.

The **Essenes** were driven by a desire to reverse assimilation and compromise with Hellenistic culture. They chose the path of withdrawal. They were not content to work within the system. They believed they alone were the true people of God. They formed an alternative community at Qumran outside of Jerusalem. The Essenes studied the Scriptures, prayed and enforced careful adherence to the Torah. They believed faithfulness to the Torah would bring God back to restore the fortunes of Israel. The Essenes did not participate in revolution. They believed that God would return, sending a priestly and kingly messiah to lead them in war against Gentiles and compromising Jews, the "sons of darkness." They believed this time to be very close, so they took the quietest path of withdrawal, ritual purity and prayer.

The **Sadducees and priests** were the official teachers of the Law and recognized representatives of mainline Jewish religion. They were members of the ruling council, the Sanhedrin, along with the Pharisees. The Sadducees depended on the favor of the Romans to get and keep their influential positions in society. They lacked a longing for change and were satisfied with maintaining a status quo and retaining power from the Romans.

The **Zealots** became a subculture within the nation. They were zealous for Israel and willing to take up arms in violent revolution. They took inspiration from the account of the old priest Mattathias of the Maccabean revolt. They were loyal to the Torah, fiercely resisted compromise with pagan culture, embraced the use of violence to achieve ends, and were willing to be martyred for the cause if necessary. The Sicarii, also known as "dagger-men," concealed knives beneath their robes to murder compromising Jewish leaders. Bands were often led by one who claimed to be the messiah. Roman authorities inevitably crushed the bands, crucified the "messiah," and savagely punished his followers. This was the fate of Judas of Galilee and his group in AD 6 and others from time to time (Mark 13:22; Acts 5:36–37). Simon the Zealot (Luke 6:15) was one of Jesus' own apostles.

Most Jews were **common people**, not part of any group, and were known as the Am ha'aretz, "the people of the land" (Hebrew: *Am* = people; ha = the article; *aretz* = land). Approximately 500,000 lived in Israel, and 3,000,000 were scattered across the Roman Empire. Many looked for when God would return and redeem his people from pagan oppressors, after which they would be free to obey the Torah and worship God in a cleansed Temple on a cleansed land. The promised Messiah was the focus. Until then, they were to be faithful so that God would speed that day. They were to learn about the Torah at synagogue and obey, celebrate festivals in their own towns and sometimes in Jerusalem, pray, keep the food laws and Sabbath, and circumcise. They were to wait in hope.

Little did they know that a young man from Nazareth, the son of a carpenter, would announce that the kingdom of God had come to Israel and was now present in him.

THE PERFECT TIME

So why was this the perfect time?

"But when the set time had fully come, God sent his Son, born of a woman, born under the law, to redeem those under the law, that we might receive adoption to sonship."
–Galatians 4:4–5

PERSIAN INFLUENCE

Prior to the Greeks and the Romans, the Persians were preparing the way for the Gospel. They created a true empire, a road system which connected the parts of the world, a postal system (Esther 3:13, 15; 8:10, 14) and a universal language, Aramaic.

THE WORLD OF IDEAS WAS DYNAMIC

Following the Persians, the world of ideas became dynamic under Alexander the Great, the greatest influence between the testaments.

He broke down the power of tradition and opened up minds to think new thoughts and make new discoveries, particularly the discovery of the individual. The Old Testament period of community and the people of God was pitted against the individual—the "tension between Jerusalem and Athens." The world of ideas was wide open for discovery of the idea of the coming of Christ and a spiritual kingdom.

JEWISH SOCIETY HAD BECOME DIVERSE

Fissures had occurred. There was no longer a monolithic, or singular type of Jewish society. In addition to Prophetic Judaism centered around the Old Testament, we see the emergence of apocalyptic Judaism, Jews that are saying the Messiah is going to come and usher in a kingdom on Earth; scribal Judaism, the Old Testament *plus* interpretive laws around the Old Testament; and secular Judaism, Jews that abandoned the faith and made Judaism only a secular culture.

Jewish society divided itself into parties and sects, including religious extremists (Pharisees and Essenes); religious moderates (Sadducees); political extremists (Zealots); political moderates (Herodians); and the Am ha'aretz, "the people of the land," Jews who did not join a party or sect to engage in the world of ideas. The Am ha'aretz were people of the soil who were content and concerned only with securing food for the table and developing their families. They were "common people," people without a shepherd, people ministered to by Jesus (Matthew 9:36).

PAX ROMANA (PEACE)

In the Pax Romana, Roman rule and law united diverse countries into one economic union (Luke 2:1). Roman roads and security allowed for commerce and travel, so people and ideas could move, including missionaries bringing the Gospel out from Jerusalem. The 200-year period of the Pax Romana was a time of peace, not military conflict. With Roman citizenship, a person could travel from country to country with freedom.

JEWISH DIASPORA

The Jews were dispersed in "Diaspora" by the Assyrians, Babylonians and Romans. The expansion of the Church and the Gospel by Paul started in the synagogue of a strategic city with a Jewish community (Acts 13 ff.). Paul's sermons were historical in a Jewish context; he started with Abraham, Isaac and Jacob, then told the people about the one who fulfilled all the aspirations of these people, Jesus Christ.

MORAL DECAY

This was a period of moral bankruptcy and decay. The times were pagan.

> *"Furthermore, just as they did not think it worthwhile to retain the knowledge of God, so God gave them over to a depraved mind, so that they do what ought not to be done. They have become filled with every kind of wickedness, evil, greed and depravity. They are full of envy, murder, strife, deceit and malice. They are gossips, slanderers, God-haters, insolent, arrogant and boastful; they invent ways of doing evil; they disobey their parents; they have no understanding, no fidelity, no love, no mercy. Although they know God's righteous decree that those who do such things deserve death, they not only continue to do these very things but also approve of those who practice them."*
>
> –Romans 1:28–32

> *"So I tell you this, and insist on it in the Lord, that you must no longer live as the Gentiles do, in the futility of their thinking. They are darkened in their understanding and separated from the life of God because of the ignorance that is in them due to the hardening of their hearts. Having lost all sensitivity, they have given themselves over to sensuality so as to indulge in every kind of impurity, and they are full of greed."*
>
> –Ephesians 4:17–19

The world was in need of a righteous savior.

Appendix B

JESUS AS THE FULFILLMENT OF THE OLD TESTAMENT

The Old Testament pointed to Jesus throughout the biblical story, not just with prophecy and prediction, but also with typology, which is the study of how Jesus is prefigured or symbolized by Old Testament persons and institutions. These institutions "lean forward" in pointing to Christ. This appendix more fully examines multiple ways in which Jesus is foreshadowed in the Old Testament.

JESUS PRESENT AT CREATION

Jesus was present at creation as Creator and Sustainer of the world, the one whom John will later tell us is also the Redeemer of the World (John 1:1–5).

JESUS AS A NEW ADAM

Just as Adam represents the start of the creation of mankind, Jesus is a new Adam, the start of a new creation in the Spirit.

Adam, when tempted, failed, and he lost the Garden for all of mankind. However, Jesus, when tempted in multiple ways, was obedient and recovered the lost Paradise for mankind.

PREDICTION OF JESUS AS REDEEMER

Genesis 3:15 provides us with the first sign of hope in which God reveals that the woman's offspring will one day defeat the serpent.

JESUS AS THE NEW ABRAHAM

When God blessed Abraham, he told Abraham that he was to start something new. Abraham's family was the start of a new nation whose name was eventually changed to Israel by the renaming of Jacob, a patriarch and father of the twelve sons who led to the tribes of Israel. However, we know the story of Israel's failure to fulfill its mission to be a light to the world. One of the ways in which Jesus revealed himself was as the Light of the World, in which he provided a pathway to bring people of all nations out of darkness and into light.

JESUS AS THE NEW ISAAC

We get our first glimpse of Jesus' substitutionary sacrifice through Abraham's willingness to sacrifice his own beloved son. God provides a substitute sacrifice, the ram caught in the thicket (Genesis 22:13–14). Jesus is the substitutionary sacrifice for our sins.

JESUS AS THE NEW ISRAEL

As the son of Abraham, Jesus is also Israel (Matthew 1:1–17).

Christ is the true spiritual seed of Abraham (Galatians 3:16).

Just as Jacob, who was renamed Israel, had 12 sons which initiated the 12 tribes of Israel, Jesus had 12 apostles and reconstituted Israel's 12 tribes (Matthew 19:28).

Matthew tells us that Jesus' return from Egypt is a fulfillment of passages of Exodus and Hosea, saying, "Out of Egypt have I called my son" (Matthew 2:15).

Just as Israel passed through the waters, Jesus went through the waters. "And a voice from heaven said, 'This is my Son, whom I love; with him I am well pleased'" (Matthew 3:17).

When Israel was tested in the wilderness for 40 days, which turned into 40 years, Israel grumbled and failed. However, Jesus was tempted in the wilderness for 40 days, and he referred to Scriptures given to Israel (Deuteronomy 8:3; 6:16; and 6:13). Jesus succeeded.

Israel was exiled, and later restored through the mercy of God. Jesus was exiled at the cross, and through his resurrection, brought about the restoration promised by the Prophets of the true Israel.

JESUS AS THE NEW MOSES

Moses was the prototypical prophet (Deuteronomy 18:15); Jesus was the ultimate prophet (John 1:1).

As author of the Torah, Moses was the prototypical Law giver. As documented in Matthew's Torah, Jesus is the ultimate Law giver: the Sermon on the Mount (chapters 5–7); the Mission Discourse (chapter 10); the Parables of the Kingdom (Matthew 13); the New Community (chapter 18); the Coming Crisis (chapters 23–25).

Just as Moses narrowly escaped an attempt on his life (Exodus 1:22–2:10), Jesus narrowly escaped an attempt on his life (Matthew 2).

Just as Moses fasted 40 days and nights (Exodus 34:28), Jesus fasted 40 days and nights (Matthew 4:2).

Just as Jesus led the people out of Egypt in the Exodus, Jesus leads us out of our spiritual exile, a Second Exodus. He came to deliver eternal salvation. He came to bring many sons to glory. He came to create co-heirs. He claimed an inheritance, to say to the Devil that these people are not rightfully yours. They belong to Jesus as his sons and daughters. He set the captives free.

JESUS AS THE NEW JOSHUA

Joshua, or *Yehoshua* in Hebrew, means "God saves." Jesus, or Yeshua, is the Greek form of Joshua. Just as Joshua led the Israelites into the Promised Land, Jesus is the new conquering King or Deliverer who restores the people to the new Promised Land.

JESUS AS THE NEW ELIJAH

Elijah's message was a prophetic rebuke of Israel (including her leaders) for pagan idolatry, especially the worship of Baal, urging Israel to turn from idolatry to follow the God of Israel (1 Kings 18:21). Jesus' message was a prophetic rebuke of religious leaders for misleading the people and for having an outward righteousness while their hearts were far from God (Matthew 23:1–39). Jesus identified himself as the Good Shepherd who lays down his life for his sheep, the giver of eternal life (John 10:1–42).

Elijah and Jesus had similar miracles. Elijah prophesied that the rain would cease for years (1 Kings 17:1) and when the rain would come (18:41–45); Jesus calmed a storm (Mark 4:35–41). Elijah multiplied oil and flour for a starving widow and her son when she was willing to share her portion (1 Kings 17:14); Jesus multiplied loaves and fish for crowds who had come to hear him when a boy was willing to share his portion (John 6:1–15). Elijah raised a widow's son from the dead (1 Kings 17:22); Jesus raised a widow's son (Luke 7:11–16), Jairus' daughter (Mark 5:35–43) and Lazarus (John 11). Jesus himself is raised from the dead as he had predicted (Luke 24:1–12).[46]

Before departing the Earth, Elisha asked to receive a double portion of Elijah's spirit, and Elijah promised it would be so if Elisha remained with him and saw him as he was taken (2 Kings 2:9–12). Likewise, Jesus noted that his followers would do greater works than he did (John 14:12), and that they would receive power from the Holy Spirit to be his witnesses (Acts 1:8).

Elijah was the only person besides Enoch whom the Bible indicates did not die. Instead, he was taken by a chariot of fire (2 Kings 2:11). Jesus ascended to heaven in the clouds as his disciples watched (Acts 1:9).

46 Jews for Jesus, "Jesus and Elijah: Comparisons and Contrasts," accessed June 6, 2012, https://jewsforjesus.org/blog/jesus-and-elijah-comparisons-and-contrasts.

JESUS AS THE NEW ELISHA

Both Elisha and Jesus:

- Were designated by a prophet, whom the general populace recognized as a true prophet
- Received the Spirit on the other side of the Jordan (2 Kings 2:7–15; John 1:28)
- Were surrounded by more disciples than their predecessors
- Were itinerant miracle workers
- Gave life in a land of death
- Cleansed lepers (2 Kings 5; Mark 1:40–45)
- Healed the sick (2 Kings 4:34–35; Mark 8:22–25)
- Defied gravity (2 Kings 6:6; Matthew 14:22–33)
- Reversed death by raising dead sons and restoring them to their mothers (2 Kings 4:1–7; Luke 7:11–17)
- Helped widows in desperate circumstances and were kinsman redeemers to save from slavery (2 Kings 4:1–7; Luke 4:19)
- Fed the hungry (2 Kings 4:1–7; Mark 8:1–12)
- Ministered to the Gentiles (2 Kings 5:1–16; Matthew 8:5–13, 28–34; 15:21–28)
- Prepared and sat at table with sinners (2 Kings 6:20–23; Luke 5:29)
- Led captives (2 Kings 6:18–20; Ephesians 4:7–8)
- Had a covetous disciple (Gehazi and Judas)
- Ended his life in a life-giving tomb from which people fled (2 Kings 13:20–21; Mark 16:1–8)[47]

---

47 The Gospel Coalition, "Elisha as a Type of Christ and His Disciples," accessed November 22, 2023, https://www.thegospelcoalition.org/blogs/justin-taylor/elisha-as-type-of-christ-and-his/.

JESUS AS THE NEW DAVID

While David was a prototypical king, Jesus was the ultimate ruler or King, greater than David and Solomon (Matthew 12; Mark 16:61–62). One of David's sons far down the genealogical tree (the one celebrated in Psalm 110:1) was actually the root underneath the whole tree, and not just the branch!

David ate showbread for his mighty men, whereas Jesus walked through the grain fields on the Sabbath, and Jesus broke bread as the sacrificial remembrance.

JESUS AS THE NEW SOLOMON

King David's son Solomon was granted wisdom. However, Jesus' wisdom was greater than Solomon's (Luke 11:14). Jesus fulfilled the coronation of Solomon (Psalm 8:5; Matthew 21:1–11). King Solomon rode to the throne on a mule (1 Kings 1:38–40). As predicted in Zechariah 9:9, Jesus rode into Jerusalem during Passion Week on a donkey (Matthew 21:1–2).

JESUS AS THE SECOND EXODUS

The prophet Hosea predicted a time when the Israelites would return from the Exodus in Egypt (Hosea 11:11). In his Gospel, John told us how Jesus would settle us into our new homes (John 14:2–3). The book of Revelation gives a glimpse into the new heaven and the new earth, with no more sea (21:1–7).

JESUS AS THE NEW COVENANT

Moses was presented the covenant at Mt. Sinai, a covenant under which the people of Israel were to live. The prophet Jeremiah predicted a new covenant with the people of Israel (Jeremiah 31:31). In his Gospel, Matthew later clarified Jesus' intent to embody mercy, not sacrifice (12:7; 9:13), and Jesus brought us into the New Covenant during the Passion Week (26:27–28).

JESUS GIVING THE NEW TORAH

Pentecost is associated with giving of the Law,[48] whereas Jesus gave us the new Law (new Torah).

JESUS AS THE ULTIMATE SABBATH

The Sabbath is a physical day, the last day of the week, that has a future meaning fulfilled in Christ. Whereas the Sabbath was given to us as a day of rest (Exodus 20:8–10), Jesus declared himself to be the Sabbath (Matthew 12:8), and he invited everyone to come to him for rest (Matthew 11:28). Joshua, quoting from Psalm 9:8–11, used the word "rest" to refer to the purpose of the Sabbath (Joshua 1:13). The book of Hebrews speaks of the ultimate Sabbath for those who follow Jesus (4:9). God's people always have a chance at any given moment to enter God's rest through faith. In his presence we can all experience eternal time.

JESUS AS THE NEW TABERNACLE AND TEMPLE

When God first dwelled with his people, it was in the Garden of Eden. The Garden had temple attributes, but there was no physical building. After the people were exiled from the Garden, God gave them instructions to build a temporary dwelling place, the Tabernacle. They later built a more permanent dwelling place, the Temple. However, as magnificent as the Temple was at times, it was destroyed twice.

There is a longstanding ancient Near Eastern idea that the temples on Earth reflected something in heaven. Old Testament institutions are not simply on the ground pointing forward, but they start on the ground as a reflection of something in heaven. The writer of Hebrews emphasizes that Jesus is actually the heavenly reality fully present on Earth. Although the Tabernacle and the Temple became the dwelling place of God in the midst of his people and typified the places and the

48 http://www.firstchurchoftheinternet.org/holidays/holidays3.htm, accessed November 11, 2014.

manner in which Jehovah met with his people and dealt with their sins, Zechariah predicted a time when a branch shall grow up out of his place and build the Temple of the Lord (Zechariah 6:12). Jesus, the Incarnate Christ, ministered directly, and predicted the replacement of the earthly Temple with himself (John 2:19). Jesus has always been the center of God's glory in heaven. Jesus brought heaven to Earth.

The Tabernacle and the Temple symbolized the body of Christ. Jesus became the new ekklesia (i.e., church, community, group of called ones) as described in Matthew 16:18; 18:15–20.

Hanukkah celebrates the rededication of the Temple. Jesus tells us that he is the ultimate eternal Temple (John 10:1–39).

JESUS AS THE ULTIMATE HIGH PRIEST/ MELCHIZEDEK

The book of Leviticus introduced us to the high priest of the community, who was anointed and ordained to make atonement for the sins of the people (16:30–33). Human priests were God-ordained representatives who were helpful for centuries. However, they were fallible. They had to make offerings for themselves.

All of the priests with all of their sacrifices were participating in a revelatory drama, act after act, that was going to be followed by a grand climax when everything that they had ever done would finally make sense.

Although Jesus was not a descendent of Levi or Aaron by blood, he is the fulfillment of the priestly role they embodied. The writer to the Hebrews also points to the somewhat mysterious figure Melchizedek who uniquely anticipated Christ as a priestly ruler in Salem (Jerusalem) with no recorded genealogy.

Hebrews tells us that Jesus was made fully human so that he could become the ultimate, merciful and faithful high priest in service to God so that he might make a "once and for all" atonement for the sins of the people by offering his own blood eternally in heaven (2:17; 4:14; 9:7, 12–14; 10:3).

JESUS AS THE ULTIMATE PASSOVER SACRIFICE

The Passover lamb is *a protective offering delivering Israel from God's judgment.* It is associated with Israel's deliverance (Exodus 12) and the Feast of Firstfruits (Leviticus 23). The Israelites were required to bring to the Lord a female lamb or goat from the flock as a sin offering, and the priest made atonement for them for their sin (Leviticus 5:6). Hebrews 10:10 tells us that we have been made holy through the sacrifice of the body of Jesus Christ once for all. Jesus was sacrificed as the ultimate and final Passover Lamb (1 Corinthians 5:7) and is considered the firstfruits of those who belong to him (15:23).

JESUS AS THE ULTIMATE PURIFICATION VESSEL

In the Old Testament, vessels which became impure, if touched, were assumed to transmit their impurity to humans, and thus had to be discarded (Exodus 30:18–19; Leviticus 14–15). Jesus, however, is the one who purifies. Purity is contagious, not impurity (John 2:1–12).

JESUS AS THE GOOD SHEPHERD

In the Old Testament and the ancient Near East in general, shepherds were protectors of their flocks. The shepherd that Israel was promised in the Old Testament was not only a Davidic king, but was God himself. God said that he would send David to shepherd his people, and he himself would tend his lambs (Ezra 34:23–24). Jesus, Son of David and Son of God, fed the multitudes and calmed the sea. Jesus was the ultimate Good Shepherd who laid down his life for his sheep (John 10:1–42).

JESUS AS THE BREAD OF LIFE

Moses was promised that the Lord would rain down bread for the people (Exodus 16:4), and that the Lord God would bring the people into a good land, a land where bread will not be scarce, and they would lack nothing (Deuteronomy 8:7–9). Jesus declared himself to be the true, sustaining bread of life (John 6:35).

JESUS AS LIVING WATER

In the ancient Near East (and still today) water was a scarce, life-sustaining commodity. Shepherds were responsible for locating and providing water for their flocks. Jesus spoke of living water, saying, "Let anyone who is thirsty come to me and drink. Whoever believes in me, as Scripture has said, rivers of living water will flow from within them" (John 7:37–38).

JESUS AS THE PREDICTED SUFFERING SERVANT

Isaiah predicted the suffering servant who would silently be led to a slaughter and take on the iniquity of us all (Isaiah 53:5–7). Jesus said that his death and resurrection would take place so that the writings of the Prophets might be fulfilled (Matthew 26:54–56).

JESUS AS SCRIPTURE

The Hebrew Bible was considered to be the Word of God. John's Gospel tells us that Jesus was the Word, and the Word was both with God and was God (John 1:1).

JESUS AS THE ULTIMATE RABBI

Rabbis were Jewish teachers of the Law who emerged in the Intertestamental Period (Matthew 23:7). Jesus was the ultimate rabbi who corrected the teaching of the Jewish rabbis (Matthew 23:8; John 3:2).

JESUS AS WATER AND LIGHT–TABERNACLES

The two major ceremonies of the Feast of Tabernacles were the water procession and the illumination of the Temple.[49] Jesus used two traditional symbols from the Feast of Tabernacles celebration, water and light, to help the people understand who he is and what he offers. Jesus referred to himself as "living water" and "the light of the world" (John 7:1–9:11).

JESUS AS THE PROMISED LAND

The Jews had been exiled from the Promised Land and later restored, after which they became corrupt again. Thus, they would again lose the Temple and be exiled from the land. In John, Jesus communicated that everything they were about to lose was him. Hebrews 4:2 states, "For we also have had the good news proclaimed to us, just as they did; but the message they heard was of no value to them, because they did not share the faith of those who obeyed."

49 Lorraine Day, "The Feast of Tabernacles," accessed November 11, 2014, http://www.goodnewsaboutgod.com/studies/spiritual/home_study/feast_of_tabernacles.htm.

Appendix C

AN ADDTIONAL STRUCTURAL LOOK AT THE BIBLE

Another common way to frame the entire Bible is into its six major content-related sections:

- The Five Books of Moses include Genesis to Deuteronomy and explores the Formation of the People of God from Eden to Canaan.
- The Historical and Poetic Books include Joshua to 2 Chronicles and Job to Song of Songs and explores the Mission of the People of God in the Promised Land.
- The Prophetic and Restoration Books include Isaiah to Malachi and Ezra to Esther and explores the Exile and Return of the People of God.

There is then a 400-year period between the testaments, called the Intertestamental Period. It is the period between Malachi, the last book of the Old Testament, and the Gospels. The history of this period is captured in writings outside the Bible.

- The Four Gospels include the life, ministry, teachings and passion of Christ, as well as the individual Gospels, and explores the Restoration of the People of God.

- Acts and the Pauline Epistles include Acts to Philemon and explores the Mission of God's People to the Nations.
- The General Epistles and Revelation include Hebrews to Revelation and explores the Sojourn of God's People Among the Nations.

STRUCTURAL PARALLELS

Let's note some structural parallels in the Bible.

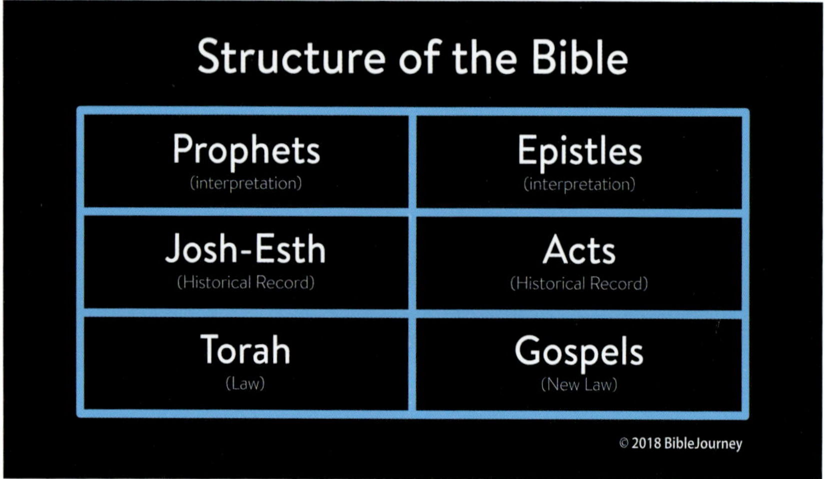

Figure C.1, Structure of the Bible

The Torah provides the foundation for the Old Testament. The Law is the basis for the covenantal relationship between God and his people. The books of Joshua through Esther provide us a glimpse of the historical record in which the people of God live out their relationship with God under the covenantal stipulations. The Prophets then sit on top of the historical record and interpret it for us. They provide two high level messages: one of warning and one of hope.

Note the New Testament parallels. In the Gospels, Jesus does not do away with the Law, but he gets right to the essence of the Law in two simple commandments. In Matthew 22:37-40, Jesus says, "'Love the Lord your God with all your heart and with all your soul and with all your mind.' This is the first and greatest commandment. And the second is like it: 'Love your neighbor as yourself.' All the Law and the Prophets hang on these two commandments."

These commandments form the basis for the relationship between God and his people in the New Testament. The book of Acts provides us a glimpse of the historical record of the New Testament. The Epistles sit on top of the book of Acts and interpret the historical record, much like the Prophets sit on top of the historical books and interpret them for us.

Appendix D

KEY TAKEAWAYS

ACT 1 CREATION: GOD ESTABLISHES HIS KINGDOM

The creation story introduces us to a transcendent God who spoke a good, ordered world into existence and gave his image-bearers their unique role.

- It is about how the world was created, not when the world was created.
- Good science and good theology are compatible.
- Creation is characterized by beauty, order and purpose.
- God spoke the world into existence.
- God created man in his own image (sets humans apart), male and female.
- We are designed to reflect and showcase God's love.
- We are designed to reflect God's loving rule as we exercise dominion over his creation.
- It is our responsibility to be fruitful and multiply.
- The triune God is revealed—Father, Son and Holy Spirit.

- The creation story is unique amongst competing ancient Near Eastern (ANE) stories.

ACT 2 THE FALL: REBELLION IN THE KINGDOM

The Fall tells us the story of two individuals who sought to become autonomous, and as a result radically altered the course of human history.

- Adam and Eve sought to become autonomous instead of depending upon their Creator for their understanding of the world and their place within it.
- The ordered world becomes chaotic.
- Consequences of the Fall in Genesis 3:
    - o Alienation from God and the Garden (vv. 8, 23)
    - o Damaged relations with each other (vv. 12, 16)
    - o Death (v. 19)
    - o Non-human creation cursed (v. 17)
    - o Creational task burdened (vv. 16–19)
- A sign of hope: the woman's offspring will one day defeat the serpent, although at great cost (Genesis 3:15).

ACT 3 REDEMPTION INITIATED: GOD CHOOSES ISRAEL

"The remainder of the Old Testament tells the story of how the Creator God called a people to be his partner in rescuing humanity and restoring all of creation."

–Dillon Thornton

- Following two additional catastrophic episodes, the Flood and the Tower of Babel, God chooses Abraham and establishes a covenant with him to continue his plan for mankind.

- Covenant promises: Abraham's descendants will become a great nation; they will possess the Promised Land; and they will be a light and a blessing to the other nations.
- The promise continues through the patriarchs.
- God rescues his people from oppression in Egypt and brings them to Mt. Sinai, where he proposes to them in his covenant with Moses and instructs them in the Law.
- God once again dwells with his people, this time in a temporary dwelling—the Tabernacle.
- God makes a covenant with David, and David unites the kingdom, and brings the Ark to Jerusalem.
- David's son, Solomon, builds the Temple on Mount Zion.
- The kingdom splits into Israel (Northern Kingdom) and Judah (Southern Kingdom).
- The people fail to fulfill their mission, the land is devastated and the Temple is destroyed, and God exiles his people through his chosen instruments: Assyria (Israel in 722 BC) and Babylon (Judah in 586 BC).
- The people return to the land 70 years later, and they rebuild the Temple and reinitiate the sacrificial system, but without a Davidic king.
- Prophets overlay messages of warning and hope during the historical books.

INTERLUDE: INTERTESTAMENTAL PERIOD (KINGDOM STORY WAITS FOR AN ENDING)

"The Intertestamental Period bridges the testaments through the preparation for the Gospel."
–Dr. Robert Cooley

- The 400 "Silent Years"—no prophetic writings between Malachi (~430 BC) and the New Testament.
- The Perfect Time:
    - o The world of ideas had become dynamic under Alexander the Great.
    - o Jewish society is divided into parties and sects.
    - o Pax Romana: Roman rule united diverse countries into one economic union.
    - o Jewish Diaspora led to dispersed Jewish communities to which Paul preached from a Jewish context (Jesus as the fulfillment of the Old Testament promises).
    - o Moral bankruptcy: moral decay; the world needed a righteous savior.

ACT 4 REDEMPTION ACCOMPLISHED: THE COMING OF THE KING

In the Gospels, the long-awaited hero, Jesus Christ, fulfills God's promise to redeem the fallen world.

- The Word became flesh (incarnation) and tabernacled among us again (John 1:14).
- Jesus selected the 12 apostles, representing the 12 tribes of Israel, to continue the mission.
- Through his death, resurrection and ascension, Jesus redeemed the world, and he reigns at the right hand of God.
- Jesus succeeded where Israel failed.
- The kingdom arrived but is not fully complete—the "already but not yet."

ACT 5 THE MISSION OF THE CHURCH: SPREADING THE NEWS OF THE KING

Although Jesus brings the kingdom of God, it does not arrive all at once. Until he comes again, Jesus commissions and empowers his followers to witness to him to the entire world.

- The Spirit descends upon the Church at Pentecost as predicted (Acts 2:21; Joel 2:28–32).
- The mission to spread the Gospel (the "good news") to the ends of the earth continues through the Church (Matthew 28:19).
- We are story dwellers, not just story tellers, uniquely equipped for our God-given purpose.

ACT 6 REDEMPTION COMPLETED: THE RETURN OF THE KING

The story ends with a new heaven and a new earth in which everything is restored, and we are once again face-to-face in the presence of the awesome Almighty.

- Jesus will return to redeem and restore all of creation.
- Revelation contains apocalyptic literature with representative symbols.
- Jesus defeats the enemy in the supernatural, spiritual realm.
- Revelation 21 gives us a glimpse into the ultimate hope for us as a follower of Christ.
- The curses of the Fall are reversed, including death itself.
- We will once again be in a Garden, dwelling face-to-face with the Almighty God in peace and unity with fellow believers and all of God's creation.

Appendix E

CHALLENGE AND REFLECTION QUESTIONS

Act 1: Do you yourself reflect God's image, and do you treat *all* others as God's image-bearers?

Act 2: What are the gods which need to be removed from your life—money, power, drugs/alcohol, work, self-esteem?

Act 3: What sin is preventing you from having the full relationship you desire with God?

Interlude: When God is silent in your prayer life, how do you respond?

Act 4: Have you accepted Jesus as Lord, not just Savior?

Act 5: How has God uniquely equipped you for your role in Act 5, what parts of your story do you see reflecting kingdom living, and how is the Holy Spirit nudging you regarding use of your spiritual gifts in the calling that God has planned for you?

Act 6: Armed with knowledge of the story, which loved ones or acquaintances do you need to reach out to and share the salvation message before it becomes too late?

ADDITIONAL REFLECTION QUESTIONS

- What did you find surprising about each part of the Bible story?
- What else did you find interesting about each part of the Bible story?
- How has each part of the Bible story challenged your thinking?
- How has each part of the Bible story shaped your worldview?
- What will you do differently as a result of what you learned?

Appendix F

GLOSSARY

Apocalypse, apocalyptic: the dramatic and climactic end of human history, to be followed by the unchallenged reign of God through his Messiah

archetype, archetypal: ultimate person, place or thing that other examples resemble

atonement: the reconciliation between sinful mankind and God through the sacrifice of Jesus Christ on the cross

autonomy: having the right or power of self-government

baptism: ritual immersion or sprinkling that marks purification and initiation

canon: authoritative collection

Christos: (Greek) anointed

Classical Prophet: a prophet whose writings are in the Bible

covenant: formalized relationship involving obligations and promises

cuneiform: an ancient Mesopotamian writing system consisting of wedge-shaped characters pressed in clay

curse: the invocation of supernatural power for a negative effect

Diaspora: the dispersed population of any ethnic group from their historical, native homeland

ekklesia: (Greek) assembly

election: selection for a divine purpose

enmity: a state of hostility or opposition

ephod: (1) sleeveless garment worn by Israel's priests; (2) religious image that functioned as an oracle

Eschatology, (-logical): the study of end times

eternality: the condition or quality of being eternal

ex nihilo: (Latin) [creation] out of nothing

exile: unwillingly removed from one's native place

Exilic Prophets: prophets who wrote during the Exile

Fall, the: the loss of paradise in the biblical story; the advent of human sin, evil and death

foreshadow: a sign or hint of things to come

Former Prophets: certain historical books in the Hebrew Old Testament (Joshua, Judges, Samuel, Kings)

genre: literary category

Hasmonean: a Jewish dynasty, descendants of the Maccabees, that ruled Judea in the second century BC.

hieroglyphics: the pictographic writing system of ancient Egypt

Intertestamental Period: the time between the writing of the final books of the Old Testament and the coming of Jesus

Latter Prophets: a subdivision of the books constituting the second main part of the Hebrew Bible, comprising those books which in Christian tradition are alone called the Prophets and which are divided into Major Prophets and Minor Prophets.

Major Prophet: prophets whose writings are longer in length (Isaiah, Jeremiah, Ezekiel and Daniel)

Messiah: Anointed One

metanarrative: overarching, interconnected storyline

Minor Prophet: prophets whose writings are shorter (Hosea, Joel, Amos, Obadiah, Jonah, Micah, Nahum, Habakkuk, Zephaniah, Haggai, Zechariah, and Malachi)

miracle(s), (miraculous): event(s) ascribed to supernatural intervention

Mishnah, (-aic): an authoritative collection of Jewish interpretive traditions from the early centuries after Christ

monotheistic: believing in a single God

myth, (-ical), (-ically), (-ology): stories about gods and goddesses that are integrated into a religious and supernatural worldview

omer: a biblical unit of measure; a dry measure for grain that is equivalent to approximately 2 quarts (imperial system) or 2 liters (metric system)

oracle: a message from the divine world to the human world, often mediated by a priest(ess) or prophet(ess)

Oral Prophets: non-literary prophets who functioned ~300 years prior to the prophets of last 17 books of Old Testament (e.g., Elijah, Elisha, Ahijah, Micaiah, Huldah)

original sin: the universal, innate, human tendency to sin, inherited from Adam as a result of the Fall

pagan: associated with non-Abrahamic religion, typically polytheistic

Pantheon: the entire system of deities within a culture or kingdom

parable: a fictional story that is laid alongside a literal reality to bring greater clarity and meaning to that reality

parallel(s): something similar to something else (e.g., poem, story, law, etc.)

patriarchal: a culture defined by male authority

Pax Romana: (Latin) Roman peace

polytheistic: believing in multiple gods

Pre-classical Prophet: a non-writing prophet who prophesied in an earlier era (Samuel, Nathan, Elijah and Elisha)

prediction: a statement about specific future events that often includes "what" and "when" elements

promise: an oath or assurance of something (e.g., a future blessing or redemption)

prophecy: a statement about the present or future that often includes words of promise and/or judgment (often follow an "if … then …" format)

prophet: God's spokesperson who called people back to their covenant relationship in the present and usually delivered a twofold message of warning and hope for the future

proto-: original, first

prototype: the initial model for subsequent developments and examples

remnant: a small remaining quantity

ritual, (-ly): a set of actions performed to a certain standard or in accord with a procedure, usually in a broadly defined ceremonial context

scroll: a roll of parchment used for writing

Second (or New) Exodus: a new divine rescue from captivity (patterned after the Exodus from Egypt)

Second Temple Period: the centuries of the rebuilt temples in Israel: 516 BC to AD 70

Sect(-arian): religious groups that have a political orientation

Septuagint: the Greek translation of the Old Testament dating to the third century BC and following; also referred to as LXX (seventy), from the story of the 72 translators who produced it

sovereignty, (sovereign): the exercise of the highest power and authority

Sukkot (Hebrew): Festival of Tabernacles

suzerain: a sovereign who has a covenant treaty with his people/ vassals

Torah: the teaching or Law given on Mt. Sinai (the complete five books of Moses)

transcendence: the state of being beyond the range of normal perception

typology: a correspondence between people, institutions, places and events

Writing Prophets: prophets whose writings are recorded in the Bible

ABOUT THE AUTHOR

Bryan Dolan is a co-founder and Chief Operating Officer of Bible Journey, a ministry to train and equip pastors, lay leaders and others in God's Word. To find out more about this ministry, go to www.biblejourney.com. He co-founded this project after spending the latter part of his career serving at a high level in the development of nuclear power facilities. During this time, the esteemed Dr. Robert Cooley mentored him after returning from the presidency of Gordon-Conwell Theological Seminary (GCTS). He helped found its Charlotte campus with Dr. Tim Laniak (PhD, Harvard), Bible Journey's co-founder.

Bryan graduated from the United States Naval Academy with a bachelor's degree in Mechanical Engineering and from Queens University with a master's degree in Business Administration. Bryan is a certified Bible teacher by GCTS and is a member of the GCTS-Charlotte Board of Advisors. Bryan brings over 40 years of business and leadership skills as an executive in the energy industry. He has also held numerous civic, church and other volunteer leadership positions. Bryan teaches the Bible in church and community settings and brings this passion to Bible Journey as we seek to engage the world in quality Bible education.